What Students Are Saying About
Major in Success

This book is so incredible that it made me feel I had the power to reach the dream job I want. Don't change a single thing. This book is very insightful.

DENISE LORD
New York, NY

I love your book. It has given me new inspiration (for) life! Dream big, keep persevering!

JOANNE HOLLSTEIN
Allison Park, PA

One of the BEST I've read on the subject. (And I have read a lot!!!)

CAROLINE FRANCIS
Lexington, KY

This is an exceptional book. It has helped me to develop my thoughts about my career aspirations and I would recommend it to everyone.

MATHEW CHRIST
Mifflinburg, PA

I could have written another book on all the things I like about *Major in Success.* I really enjoyed this book and found it very motivating and resourceful. The writing was excellent. Not only was it easy for a college student to read and relate to, but it was also humorous and inspiring. I seem to want to say a lot about your book and tell others all about it, but all I can do is recommend it to, or buy it for, friends.

DAVID FOUST
San Francisco, CA

Inspirational. I cannot put this book down. This is just what "want-to-be-successful people" need for guidance and direction. I needed this book ten years ago as a struggling freshman. I graduated and thought the degree was all I needed. Now, I am back in school pursuing my dream career. Thanks, Patrick, for sharing the tips most people don't or won't.

DEBRA RUGG
Norfolk, NE

One of the coolest books I have ever read, it kicks butt. It was the same feeling I got from seeing (the movie) *Jerry Maguire*, which I found very inspiring with substance and lessons on life. I don't know what to say, but WOW.

ANGELA TONG
New York, NY

I consider (*Major in Success*) my bible to getting the job I want. The book is excellent. I would recommend it to anyone!

JEANNIE GORECKI
Cleveland, OH

I charged a girl ten bucks for a kiss. She paid me with your book, which she swears cost $9.95. Now we're in love.

EDWARD BERLEN
Milford, PA

I have never written to (an) author before, but I truly enjoyed reading your book. It taught me so much, and I wish that I had found it a long time ago. When I read all the success stories that you included in the book, I got really excited.

VORATHEE SCOTT
Arlington, VA

This book was very inspiring. For the first time I read a book from cover to cover with no breaks. I just couldn't put it down.

ERIC ZACH
Lincoln, NE

This is the first book that I can honestly say inspired me about my future. After reading it, I was excited about my future. I can relate to you!!

MICHELLE NAVA
Vallejo, CA

I love your book! It inspired me to do things I thought I would never do. I admire you a great deal. I never knew what I wanted to do until I read *Major in Success*. Now there is not a doubt in my mind. I can't thank you enough. Thanks so much. This book is awesome.

MEGAN BASHAM
Dallas, TX

Your book is one of the best I've read on how to be successful not only in school, but also later on in my chosen profession. Your book has given me a tremendous amount of motivation to go out and do the things that will make me a valuable asset to my university and my future employers. Keep up the great work!

DONALD GASTER
College Station, TX

This is one of the most helpful books I've ever read. Because of this book I now have my major. I also have a great idea of what I want to do for the next four years of college.

CORRY HYER
Kingston, RI

This book is one of the most fascinating books . . . I own. It gave me so many tips that I would have never received in any of my classes. I've learned more from this book than I have from any of my classroom textbooks.

FALGUNI PATEL
Kenmore, NY

I'm going to keep this book by my bed at college.

TRACEY BLOTCKY
Dallas, TX

Fantastic! This book helped ease my nerves after turning down admissions offers to attend law school. I intend to follow my bliss and become a college professor. I wish I'd read your book before I started college. Great book!

COURTNEY NEWMAN
Ashland, OR

This book got me really psyched and confident that I will be able to succeed in becoming a TV producer.

HOLLY JERSPERSEN
Granville, OH

I just finished this book of yours and I must commend you. The last few chapters blew me away. And the Focus chapter kicked my ass. I've been trying to verbalize this idea about talent and that it's not something . . . you're born with. And you totally summed it up—if you just focus on what you care about, then you become talented. That's so true.

SCOTT LEBERECHT
Cincinnati, OH

Major in Success

3RD EDITION

Make College Easier, Fire Up Your Dreams,
and Get a Very Cool Job

PATRICK COMBS

TEN SPEED PRESS
Berkeley   Toronto

To my mother, Nancy "Mom" Combs, to whom I owe my most excellent upbringing. Mom, you taught me the most valuable lessons of all—"You can be anything you want;" "Don't worry about your mistakes;" "Be kind to others;" and "Look it up, that's what I bought the encyclopedias for."

To Deborah Lowe, the world's best professor. Deborah, the gifts you gave me keep on giving from the pages of this book. Thank you for so much.

TEN SPEED PRESS
P.O. Box 7123
Berkeley, CA 94707
www.tenspeed.com

Distributed in Australia by Simon & Schuster Australia, in Canada by Ten Speed Press Canada, in New Zealand by Southern Publishers Group, in South Africa by Real Books, in Southeast Asia by Berkeley Books, and in the United Kingdom and Europe by Airlift Book Company.

Text design by Jeff Brandenburg/ImageComp

Library of Congress Cataloging-in-Publication Data on file with the publisher.

First printing this edition 2000
Printed in Canada

2 3 4 5 6 — 04 03 02 01 00

Table of Contents

Special Thanks iv
Foreword by Dr. Jack Canfield v
Introduction vii

Part 1: Dream Job 1
    Chapter 1:   On the Road to Greatness 3
    Chapter 2:   Truly Passionate 8
    Chapter 3:   Major Excitement 13
    Chapter 4:   No McJobs! 15
    Chapter 5:   Money Matters 21
    Chapter 6:   Your Ultimate Life 27
    Chapter 7:   The Six Big Fears 34

Part 2: Action Plan 43
    Chapter 8:   Great Escapes 45
    Chapter 9:   Work Hard, Play Hard 52
    Chapter 10: Never Mind the Grades 58
    Chapter 11: Classes Worth Their Weight in Gold 65
    Chapter 12: More, Better, Faster, Digital 70
    Chapter 13: Excel-eration Training 73
    Chapter 14: A Major Shortcut 78
    Chapter 15: Life-Changing Reality Checks 83
    Chapter 16: Really Get Into It 86
    Chapter 17: Show-and-Tell 93
    Chapter 18: Going Pro 98
    Chapter 19: School Without an Internship Can Get You Nowhere 105
    Chapter 20: The Surefire, Nine-Step, Ultra Interview Plan 113
    Chapter 21: Future-Perfect Planning 119
    Chapter 22: Now Get Out There! 122

Part 3: High Octane 129
    Chapter 23: Focus—and Focus on What You Care About 131
    Chapter 24: Make Bold Decisions 134
    Chapter 25: Commit Yourself to Taking the Time to
                   Make Your Dreams Come True 137
    Chapter 26: Break Through Your Failures 140
    Chapter 27: Pay Yourself 10% First and Always 144
    Chapter 28: Be Good to Others 147
    Chapter 29: Bon Voyage! 151
    Chapter 30: Choices That Pay Off 153

Bonus Appendix: Tips for Teachers, Artists, Exchange Students, and Athletes 165

Special Thanks

My thanks to the following people: Lisa Marlow for helping me the very most. Mike and Anne, for your rock solid support. Lisa Ryers and Jo Ann Deck for the book deal, great ideas, and great energy. Alexis Brunner, who helped make this book happen in good speed with a minimum of fuss. Lenny Dave for the comics and enthusiasm. Scott Edelstein for the agenting. John Marlow for the constant supply of good articles and good advice. Christian Haren for teaching me the difference between admirable and enviable. Michael Combs for Total Recall. And the following people for their valuable encouragement and help: Marianne Marlow, Donald Asher, Donald Casella, Ellis Gold, Deborah Sorensen, Tamy Snyder, Christa Neilsen, Andrea Kasten, Christy Svalstad, Rita Keilholtz, Jennifer Monges, Carol Dawson, Jessica Snelling-Defilippo, Sonia Borg, Jack King, and Joe Bove.

The following people for sharing with me and contributing their inspiring stories: Michael Bates, Wendy Kopp, Veronica Chambers, Karen Socher, Amon Rappaport, David Eggers, Gilman Louie, Nancy Collins, Tabitha Soren, David Greene, Tiffany Shlain, Andrew Shue, Simon Tonner, Mike Roth, Christian Haren, Richard Thau, Lisa Miller, Chris Lindquist, Jennifer Scully, Dion Thompson, John Santos, Fidel Vargas, Diana Davila, Dudley and Sherry Ann Lynch, Robin Honig, Amy Carden, Chris McNally, Michael Elliot, Marcus Allen, Tracy Handwerk, Ben Wittowski, Andrew Limardo, Darron Trobetsky, and Robert Valadez.

Special thanks to the people who beta-tested this book: Steve Montano, Brian Fields, Nancy Fields, Stephanie Yee, Butch Lovelace, Nancy Meutz, Dwayne Lee, Andrea Cheung, and Amy Francetic.

Thanks also to the people who helped me write the Choices That Pay Off chapter: Angela M. Klueber, Christina L. Graham, Liz Kearney, Gilbert R. Gonzales, Kylae Jordan, Ireneo Ray C. Pinpin Jr., Annie Wallace, Vanessa Arteaga, Tiffany Christine Marshall, Amy Evans, Patti O'Healy, Tatiana Armstrong, Spencer Baum, Dean J. De Milio, Peter Jackson, Josh Popowski, and my fantastic editor Aaron Wehner.

Special thanks to Aaron Sherer, who helped me revise the book in 1997.

Very special thanks to Jack Canfield for doing the foreword. Troy Stende for helping me make the millennium edition hotter, cooler, and better. Michelle Watson for knowing all the great sites on the Web. My wonderful wife, Deanna Latson, for adding touches of improvement in many places. Glenn Van Ekeren, author of *The Speaker's Sourcebook II,* for going out of his way to provide me with the research by Srully Blotnick. Julie Bennett for being an awesome editor. Dan Galvin for overflowing my cup with cool quotes.

This Book Can Transform Your Future

Foreword by Jack Canfield, co-author of the *Chicken Soup for the Soul* series

You're about to read a book about true success—success in college, in your career, and in life.

But it's not your usual book about getting good grades and landing a high-paying job. For Patrick Combs, that's not nearly enough. And he hopes that once you've read the first few pages of this book, it won't be enough for you, either.

Major in Success is about living a radically successful life. This means landing (or creating) your dream job right out of college, or soon thereafter. It means living a life that brings you real joy, meaning, and satisfaction—not just a good-paying job. And, most importantly, it means starting to fulfill your dreams *right now*—not months or years down the road.

I know Patrick's approach and principles work, for several reasons. First, because people who follow Patrick's guidance radically succeed—in some cases beyond their wildest dreams. (This new edition of *Major in Success* contains many of these people's real-life stories.)

Second, because Patrick has walked his talk. By the age of 28, he was already working at his own dream job as a speaker on college campuses, writing books and columns on the side, and living the life he had envisioned for himself.

Third, because Patrick has a well-earned and well-deserved reputation as a speaker and writer. He has shared his wisdom, encouragement, and energy with tens of thousands of students at hundreds of colleges and universities around the country. His award-winning Web site, www.goodthink.com, has inspired hundreds of thousands of people of all ages. And the first two editions of *Major in Success* have helped an untold number of students get a jump-start on creating the lives they most want to live.

And fourth, I know from my own experience that what Patrick writes is true. Of course, *Major in Success* wasn't available back when I was in college (though I wish it had been). Nevertheless—through intuition, grace, or blind luck—I was fortunate enough to have followed many of Patrick's principles, and they have made an enormous difference in my life. One of the most important of these, for me, was focusing on what I loved to do; another was persisting in spite of my fears and failures.

I'm living proof of how important these principles can be. It may surprise you to know that the first volume of *Chicken Soup for the Soul* was rejected by quite a few New York presses before finding a home with a small publisher in Florida. If Mark Victor Hansen (my co-author) and I had given in to our fears—or had agreed with the unenthusiastic publishers in New York—none of the Chicken Soup books would have been published.

Fortunately, with this new edition of *Major in Success,* you have the chance to benefit from everything Patrick has to offer. So turn the page and let Patrick show you how you can live your dreams, become the person you most want to become, and get on the fast track to your own greatness.

JACK CANFIELD
February 1999

Introduction

The college system assumes that knowledge is power. But knowledge isn't power. The ability to put knowledge to use is power.

This book was written especially for all the students who feel similar to the sophomore who told me:

> *I came to college and thought it was going to teach me everything I needed to know. And I'm the kind of student who reads all my assignments, goes to class, really listens and works hard at my homework. But two years into it I'm beginning to realize that college isn't teaching me what I need to know—just like high school didn't. And I'm afraid that if I don't do something different, I'm going to graduate with very little helpful knowledge.*

You can be as successful as you want. You can get your dream job and you can establish your ideal lifestyle. You'll see evidence for this throughout the pages of this book in the stories of ordinary students who have gone on to get their dream jobs because of a few good moves they made while they were still in school.

But you are at risk! Consider the fact that research done during the last decade revealed that upwards of 70 percent of all white collar workers are dissatisfied with their jobs. In other words, most college grads are ending up in jobs they don't like—jobs that don't light their fire.

This may come as a shock to you since most students are under the impression that picking a suitable major, getting high grades, and completing a degree will result in a good job. But that promise is simply not true. People who graduate with honors are ending up in jobs they dread.

Remember not all the faculty have all their faculties.
1,001 Logical Laws by John Peers

Most of us have lives too small for our spirits.
Studs Terkel

Simply put: College won't teach you how to fire up your career. Because you are at risk, *Major in Success* is loaded with suggestions that virtually ensure that you'll get a great job at graduation by providing you with a simple, powerful success plan which will move you out of the "risk" category and into a good life.

Here's another bonus: *Major in Success* is designed to alleviate one of the biggest problems you and a million other college students face—feeling uncertain about why you're attending college at all.

People end up in college for a lot of different reasons: because they want a good education, because they wanted to get away from their parents, because everyone else was going, because their parents insisted, because it's what their siblings did, etc. But shortly into the first semester, many students begin to ponder the questions, "Why am I here?" "Am I here to get good grades?" "Am I here to build a career?" "Am I

Duel of the non-marketable.

supposed to just learn all I can from my professors?" "Or to get a credential?"

Why *are* you in college? One good reason is that ultimately, college will give you the opportunity to *increase the quality of your life,* both now and in the future. Unfortunately, a lot of students do little, if anything, to actively increase the quality of their lives while they're in school. Many students seem to think that college is some kind of a rehearsal and they won't start improving their lives until after they graduate. They don't seem to realize that life isn't a rehearsal—and neither is college.

From day one when you start college your future resume has started to take shape, whether you're working to put anything impressive on it or not. Your career is already being determined, whether or not you're directing it. Even your lifestyle is already taking shape, whether or not you're consciously trying to shape it the way you want it to be.

The fact is that it's dangerous to be in college, as a lot of students are, just to achieve in academics. There's the danger of focusing only on classroom learning because once you're in the work world, you will be required to have real-world experience. Moreover, as you'll see later on in the book, you can get good grades but still not be able to get a good job. On the other hand, it is also detrimental to focus only on getting a job while you're in school because, even though you may become a great candidate for employment, college itself does have a lot to offer.

The most dangerous way to approach college is with the idea that all you need to do is pay your dues and get your degree. If you approach college with this mindset you are shooting yourself in both feet. After graduating, you'll discover that you were paying dues to get into a club of people who missed the point. The point is that you're not in college to work for your professors, or your parents, or anyone else. You're there to work for *yourself* and your future.

Working for yourself and for your future is the central focus of *Major in Success.* The book isn't just geared to get you a job. Neither is it geared to get you good grades, nor to make college fun, or to expand your horizons, or to help you develop your talents. It's not even aimed at helping you get the most out of college. *Major in Success* is set up to help you increase the quality of your life, during college and after college. Better still is that almost every tip in the book is good for your career and good for your academics.

You will have to learn seven to ten different jobs to remain employable throughout your lifetime.

Everybody needs some inspiration,
Everybody needs some motivation,
mix it up with some imagination,
and use your natural gifts,
You've got natural gifts.
Lyrics from "Natural Gifts" by The Kinks

Granted, the book may seem like it's mostly about setting up for a fulfilling career. That is a primary conversation throughout this book and it's no accident. Consider the fact that after graduating from college you will work 70 percent of your waking hours for the next forty-some years. There's no getting around it. Unless you win the lottery or happen to have been born filthy rich, your career will be most of what you do during your life.

The good news is that there are a lot of people who have found ways to establish careers doing the things that make them happy and fulfilled. Their stories, as well as suggestions for creating success in your own life, are in this book.

I'll be describing how to set yourself up for success in detail, complete with step-by-step instructions, later on in the book. But here's a quick preview of what a success plan looks like.

You kind of have a very short window, which is your four years of college to go crazy, and everyone should go crazy in their life.

Chris Miller, co-author
of Animal House

Don't worry about moving slowly, worry about standing still.

Chinese proverb

I don't know if Mom was right or Lieutenant Dan—if we both have a destiny or if we're all floating accidentally like on a breeze, but I think maybe it's both.

Forrest Gump

1. Go to college

The first step toward success is to get into college because college really is the best place you can go to learn, practice, and make something of yourself. College is rich in resources, people, advisors, and learning tools. And in our society, a diploma is the piece of paper that gives you access to better jobs. But yeah, yeah, yeah, you already know college is a good thing to do but you also know that college doesn't necessarily result in a great job. You've seen how many college graduates are struggling to find meaningful employment. That's why there are three more steps to being successful.

2. Discover what kind of work you enjoy

The second step is to get a clear sense of what naturally motivates you the most and then develop a picture of the jobs that suit your interests. Accomplish this part of the plan and you'll be able to direct all your enthusiasm toward accomplishing your dreams. Skip this step and you're a candidate for getting a job you hate which makes you feel like a slave.

3. Do things that get the ball rolling

The third step is to acquire the knowledge and experience that will qualify you for your dream job. There are a surprising number of things you can do toward this end during college. As you accomplish these things, your confidence increases, your success speeds up, and your value in the working world goes through the roof.

If your goal is to have your own life, don't lean up against a wall waiting for someone to recognize you.
Andrew Shue, actor

If you are who you want to be you'll make it allright
You won't find a way to be free if you never try
Lyrics from the song "Life's for Living" by Jerry Wagers

It is the first of all problems for a man to find out what kind of work he is to do in this universe.
Thomas Carlyle, essayist and historian

4. Master the habits that make you unstoppable

The last step in the plan is where the rubber meets the road. The previous three steps are like training and preparing for a race. In the last step you start running and give it your best shot. When you're at this phase in the plan, things will look very different. You'll have different options to choose from and you'll see many possible routes to your dream job. You'll also have acquired many of the skills, traits, and abilities that will get you to the job of your dreams—and ultimately provide you with a meaningful life.

As you can see, it's not a complicated path to success, but it does focus on what's really important: *motivation, skills, abilities, resources, credentials,* and *your dreams.* It's the same path that got many former college students to where they wanted to be, including David Letterman, Katie Couric, Tom Hanks, Oprah Winfrey, Robin Williams, Nancy Collins, Bill Gates, and Tabitha Soren. In the next part of the book, for example, you'll learn:

- How Tabitha Soren landed her dream job co-anchoring MTV news;

- What finally convinced Tom Hanks to pursue acting;

- How Katie Couric got to the *Today Show*;

- What David Letterman did during college to get his start in television;

- What enabled John Singleton to direct his own movie just out of college;

- How Jay Leno got past a major setback and ended up hosting the *Tonight Show*;

- How celebrity interviewer Nancy Collins got her first big interview during her senior year in college;

- How David Duchovny finally figured out he wanted to be an actor;

- The step Conan O'Brien took during college that put him on track to his TV show;

- How Marcus Allen overcame his biggest fear.

to be nobody but yourself—in a world which is doing its best, night and day, to make you like everybody else—means to fight the hardest battle which any human being can fight, and never stop fighting.

e.e. cummings, poet

In addition, you'll also find inspiring stories of lesser-known recent graduates who did well for themselves by making choices you'll probably see as possible for yourself. You'll learn about:

- David Greene, who ended up being part owner of a company because of one informational interview;

- Randy Kelson, who got his dream job playing video games because he decided to call the company that made his favorite games;

- Veronica Chambers, who got her own column in a nationally circulated magazine during college by cold calling from the New York phone book;

- Wendy Kopp, who established a major national non-profit organization just after college because she turned her senior paper into a business plan;

- Michael Elliot, who got his dream job in Hollywood with a quick trip to his career center;

- Tiffany Shlain, who was able to make award-winning films during and after college by seeking out her own mentors.

You don't need to read this book as a list of tasks you should be doing while you're in college. Instead, look at it as offering possibilities to explore in your own life. It is a reality that all of us can be great at something. And although the entire book is about succeeding both professionally and academically, let me repeat the underlying philosophy of *Major in Success*: Do things that increase your enjoyment of life.

So start the book and enjoy.

> To improve the golden moment of opportunity and catch the good that is within our reach is the great art of life.
>
> *Samuel Johnson, author*

PART 1

Dream Job

I hope to die young at a very old age.
Anonymous

CHAPTER 1

On the Road to Greatness

You've got to get a kick out of whatever
you're doing. I'd rather see you as a happy
UPS driver enjoying your customers than a
miserable senior accountant at a Fortune
500 company making $70,000 a year. You
only get one trip around so you've got to
enjoy what you do and who you do it with.

Tom Peters, management expert

Think of the students around you. What personal characteristic do you think will make the difference between those who become great at something and those who never rise above mediocrity? Intelligence? Family background? Confidence?

The answer is surprising. Benjamin Bloom, a professor at the University of Chicago, recently studied 120 outstanding athletes, artists, and scholars. He was looking for the common denominators of greatness and mastery. The study concluded that intelligence and family background were NOT important characteristics for achieving mastery of a desired skill. The only characteristic that the 120 outstanding people had in common was extraordinary drive.

Extraordinary drive is the primary characteristic that powered Jay Leno through 22 years of stand-up comedy before being chosen to succeed Johnny Carson. It's the quality that took Katie Couric from her first job out of college as a desk assistant for ABC, making coffee and answering phones, to the position of cohost of the NBC *Today Show*. It's also the primary quality that enabled John Singleton to write three full-length movie scripts during college, one of which was his hit movie, *Boyz N the Hood*.

I never worked at anything that wasn't fun. If I had my life to live over I don't think I'd change a thing, except maybe to take up mountain climbing.
AC Gilbert, gold medal pole-vault champion 1908, self-made millionaire, and creator of the Erector Set

Anything you do, you better enjoy it for its true value. Because people are going to second-guess everything you do.
Bill Gates

3

I really think I've been successful because I loved the job. I like reporting, I like interviewing people. I never wanted to be a famous journalist, I wanted to be a good journalist, respected by my peers.

Katie Couric,
cohost of NBC's Today Show

The real secret of success is enthusiasm.

Walter Chrysler, entrepreneur

Profound joy of the heart is like a magnet that indicates the path of life.

Mother Teresa, nun

Most successful people enjoy their work. The real issue is not what's "hot" but what you like to do.

Jeffrey Allen, writer

Extraordinary drive is exactly what you need to succeed. . . . "Extraordinary drive" is the magic ingredient that will make your dreams come true. . . . All you need is a little "superhuman ambition" and the pot of gold at the end of the rainbow is yours! Well then, maybe you'd like to know where extraordinary drive comes from. EXTRAORDINARY DRIVE COMES FROM DOING WHAT YOU ENJOY. Doing what you love. Going with your strongest interests. Trying for your deepest aspirations.

There is research that proves the power of doing what you enjoy. Srully Blotnick focused his study on middle class workers and published his results in his book *Getting Rich Your Own Way.* Fifteen hundred people were asked about the career goals they'd set for themselves and then followed for 20 years. Eighty-three percent chose their career based on making the most money. They hoped to get rich fast in order to later do work they really wanted to. Seventeen percent of the workers chose their careers out of passion—figuring they would worry about the money later. At the end of 20 years, there were 101 millionaires from the entire group. All but one of the millionaires—100 out of 101—were from the 17 percent who had chosen to follow their passion. The other 83 percent who were trying hard to get rich fast spent 20 years making only modest earnings, in jobs they didn't particularly like. On the other hand, whether they ended up a millionaire or not, almost all the passion-driven workers enjoyed long careers in jobs they found "profoundly absorbing."

Why doing what you enjoy is so powerful

Doing what you enjoy propels you to success. How it propels you to success is simple. Success in any endeavor takes a lot of work, and the key to doing a lot of work is liking what you're working on. In the words of author and Stanford University professor Michael Ray, "You know that you are practicing your true vocation when you love all the hard work, responsibility, and tedium that goes with it." Actress Daryl Hannah put it this way, "Acting is my calling. Believe me, if I didn't feel that sense of commitment about it, I wouldn't stay in this business, because there's so much about this life that I don't like."

Remember the 20-year study of middle class workers? Mr. Blotnick had his own theory why those who followed their passions got so rich. He noticed that the passion-driven workers changed jobs at first very often, trying to find work that was truly absorbing. Because of so much job changing the passion-driven workers quickly developed a vast reservoir of knowledge and experience, and were paid much more.

Following your passions gives you the power to work hard and it rapidly develops your talents.

I have personally learned what a strong difference focusing on what you enjoy makes. My first year in college, I had no sense of the subjects that really interested me—so I ended up in many classes that bored me to death, one of which was Elements of Nuclear Physics. (Hey, it sounded impressive.) I quickly learned the results of trying to focus on things that don't interest you—I didn't even turn in my final paper that was worth 50% of my grade! I wanted to be a good student but I found the subject so uninteresting that I couldn't get the final paper done.

Luckily, a few years into college I discovered that I had a strong interest in new technology and hi-tech toys. I loved to read about it, know about it, and be around it. I was an intern at Levi Strauss & Co. when my boss was assigned to set up a videoconferencing system for the company. Videoconferencing! I'd seen it in futuristic movies before and I remembered it as being like a wall-sized TV-phone system that allowed you to talk to people in faraway places just like they were right there in the same room!

We were at lunch when I overheard that he was going to be in charge, and my heart started beating, and my mind started racing with the dream that I could help on the project. When I got back to campus that evening, I went straight to the library to look up videoconferencing articles. I spent the next seven evenings in the library and gathered more than 50 articles and photocopied pages from six books. Then

You really have to work hard to let what you are come through.
Oprah Winfrey, talk show host

You can be just like me. Don't just pussy foot around and sit on your assets. Unleash your ferocity upon an unsuspecting world.
Bette Midler

God gave me a special talent to play the game, . . . maybe he didn't give me a talent, he gave me a passion.
Wayne Gretzky

If we did all the things we were capable of doing, we would literally astound ourselves.
Thomas Edison

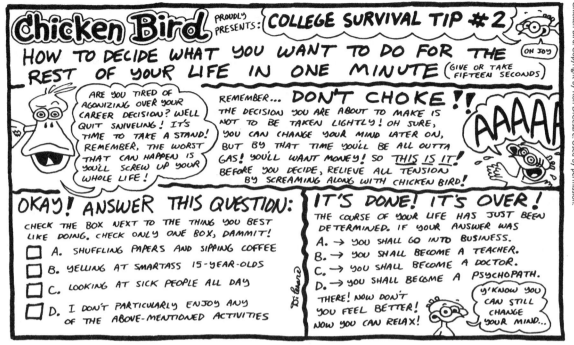

Competitiveness is silly. There's enough to go around for everybody and fate is always, always working.

Drew Barrymore

I studied the articles, organized them into a three-ring binder, and took it into Levi Strauss & Co. I set the big black binder on my boss's desk and said, "Maybe this will be helpful in that new videoconferencing project you're going to be in charge of and I'd love to help on it if you need any." His mouth dropped open in amazement as he flipped through the many articles and he finally looked up and said, "Well, you obviously know more about videoconferencing than I do" (long pause) "and you obviously have a lot of enthusiasm for the subject. How would you like the job as Levi's video-conferencing manager?" My heart probably skipped five beats. When I could recapture my breath I gladly accepted the job and he informed me that my salary would jump from $10 an hour to $25. I thought I'd retire in three months on that salary (at that time in my life my $10 an hour seemed high).

That is the power of doing what you enjoy! My love for new technology gave me the energy to do seven consecutive evenings of library research. If it had been a subject I didn't care about, you couldn't have dragged me into the library. In addition to giving me a tremendous amount of energy, my enthusiasm for the subject matter sent my boss a clear signal that said, "This person would have a lot of good energy for this position." Doing what you enjoy gives you energy and enthusiasm.

Most of us haven't been taught how to discover what we truly enjoy. As a man pointed out to me, "In other countries they tell you what to be when you grow up. In our country they only say, 'You can be anything you want.'" Well, how in the world do you figure out what you want to be?! That subject is next.

Discovering your best

I overheard a conversation between two students in a university library one afternoon. The young woman said to the young man, "We're out of here next semester—graduation came so fast." The young man replied, "Yeah, and I still don't know what I want to do for a job. How about you?" Her answer was, "I'm not sure either. I'd like to do something in communications, but I'm not sure what."

Holy hardship, Batman! Graduating without a clear picture of the kind of work you'd enjoy is like getting ready to sky-dive without a parachute—you're guaranteed a hard landing! You can't count on your college courses to reveal much about real-world jobs, so the first thing this book will walk you through is the Quick-Fast, Usually Works, Four-Step Way to Figure Out Your Best Work:

1. Admit what REALLY interests you.

2. Pinpoint your true aspirations.

3. Discover that there are many types of jobs that are related to your interest.

4. Feel your fears and do it anyway.

We act as though comfort and luxury were the chief requirements of life, when all that we need to make us really happy is something to be enthusiastic about.
Charles Kingsley, poet

My advice is to live your life. Allow that wonderful inner intelligence to speak through you.
Bernie Siegel, psychologist and writer

You've got to be very careful if you don't know where you are going, because you might not get there.
Yogi Berra, baseball player

I'll never reach my destination
If I never try
So I will sail my vessel
'Til the river runs dry
Garth Brooks, Lyrics from The River

CHAPTER 2

Truly Passionate

I didn't become an actor to develop
a personality cult or to get power over
people. I went into this because it's fun,
because it's a great way to make a living.

Tom Hanks, actor

I really didn't know what I wanted
or what moved me beyond
basketball or sex. Those were two
things that were very black and
white to me, where I could feel in
the moment.

David Duchovny

I think it is possible to value
yourself enough to say, my self
is unique. There's never been
anybody like me. Therefore, it is my
duty on this earth to manifest that
self in a unique way.

David Duchovny

In the awesome book *Before They Were Famous* by Karen Hardy Bystedt, actor David Duchovny, of the *X-Files*, talked about his college days. He was an A student and a good basketball player. "I was kind of drifting along, which might seem like a weird thing to say because I was seemingly doing so well. I was talented in a bleak way and I was just scared shitless that I wasn't going to be the best at what I was doing. But I didn't know what I wanted to do," he said. "From the ages of 5 to 20, I'd always list that I wanted to be a lawyer or a doctor on all those tests they give you, but what I really wanted to be was a basketball player." But a basketball career didn't happen; his hands were too small and after college he took a year off and bartended. "I applied for scholarships thinking that if I continued to be a student I could somehow put off defining myself." Scholarships got him into Yale but he went there still scared and undecided about what to do with his life. Then something happened. David made friends with Yale drama students and was soon inspired to write a play. "I started writing a play, and in order to learn more about writing I decided to take an acting class. In acting, I felt like I was playing ball again." His acting career started there, and within months he was in his first commercial.

First and foremost, take note about a detail in Duchovny's story. He didn't figure out his passion for acting until he was in grad school. That brings up the most important point in this chapter about figuring out your passions:

MOST PEOPLE DON'T DISCOVER WHAT THEY'RE TRULY PASSIONATE ABOUT UNTIL AFTER COLLEGE, MUCH AFTER. THIS IS PERFECTLY FINE.

I discovered my true passion for public speaking, but not until I was 26; four years after college. During college I was bouncing around like a pinball, interested in all kinds of jobs. If you figure out your dream job by 26 or even 30 you'll still be more fortunate than most. Don't worry if you haven't figured out your dream job. Instead, focus on taking the actions that will lead you to your discovery. Do this and your dream job will find you.

The actions to take are really quite straightforward and simple. But most of us have never been taught them.

The way to start recognizing your passions is surprisingly simple: Start trusting your instincts and noticing the way your mind and body react to different subjects. When you have passion for something, you're alert; you're tuned in; your mind and body are engaged; your curiosity is piqued; your adrenaline might rush a little; time passes quickly; and you love to learn more about the subject. When you're not as interested, you get bored; your mind wanders; or you tune out. A note of caution here: Getting bored, daydreaming, and tuning out are also signs of a bad teacher, a complex subject, a lack of sleep, a full stomach, or a hangover.

Truly, your own internal instincts are the best indicators you've got. Trust your own reactions—they are your best guides to enjoyment, fulfillment, satisfaction, and success. How did Tom Hanks know that acting was a passion? In his own words, "I signed up for a drama class and tried out for the plays, and got into them, and had more fun than I could possibly imagine."

More than anything else, people seek happiness.
Mihaly Csikszentmihalyi, author of Flow: The Psychology of Optimal Experience (HarperCollins)

Life is short. Live it up!
Nikita Khrushchev, premier of former U.S.S.R.

An activity becomes creative when the doer cares about doing it right, or better.
John Updike, writer

The interesting thing is that there are so few important decisions. You don't have to go in the "right" direction. You don't have to enter the "right" business. What you have to do is have made a decision as to what you're going to do and then you just have to figure out how to succeed at it.
Ken Oshman, electrical engineer

Magazines:

Artist's Ways
Astronomy
Audio Video Interiors
Business Week
Culinary Trends
Dance
Discover
Electronic Gaming
Farm and Ranch Living
Homes and Gardens
Martial Arts
Mother Jones
Muscle and Fitness
Natural Health
New Music
Organic Gardening
Outside
Personal Transformation
Photography
Premiere
Road and Track
Sports Illustrated
This Old House
Traveler
Wired
Writers and Poets

Never wanted to be like
everybody else.
*Lyrics from "Working at
the Factory" by The Kinks*

For the most part I do the thing
which my own nature drives me
to do.
Albert Einstein

The ability to give our unique
gifts to the world comes from
following our own path.
Justine and Michael Toms

To get an immediate sense of something you're passionate about look at the list of magazines in the margin and pick the ONE you think would be the COOLEST to read for one year.

If there's some other magazine that you think of as the coolest then so be it. In any case, when you've made your pick, you'll have a great indication of what you have passion for. The magazine you think is cool might lead you to your dream job (more on that in a couple of chapters). The most successful people in the world choose a job because they think it's cool. On the other hand, a lot of students will make the mistake of picking a job because it's practical—the bummer equivalent of having to write research papers about a magazine you don't like, forty hours a week.

One more thing on the magazines—it's what you would choose TODAY that matters. Don't worry about if it will be your next "passion of the month." Here and now are what matters!

If too many subjects really motivate you

When Bill Gates, the president of Microsoft Corp., was in college, he had a very hard time deciding which subject was his favorite. In his own words: "When I was in college, it was really hard to pick a career, because everything seemed so attractive, and when you had to pick a specific one you had to say no to all the others." When this is your predicament, you can reflect on these concepts:

- College is a time for exploring as many interests as you can.

- Most of all, you want to graduate with an enthusiasm for learning. You increase your enthusiasm by exploring your interests. You decrease your spirit for learning by focusing on what other people say you should focus on. In other words, you'd be better off exploring your own interests in the library than sleeping through a class that bores you.

- Choosing one subject to base your career on does not mean ignoring the others. It means relegating them to hobbies until you can incorporate them into your career.

- Some of the most successful careers have been formed by people who combined divergent interests in a new way.

- You will always be interested in many subjects simultaneously. Your job is to find ways to combine your interests toward a single purpose.

- If you're overloaded with career ideas you'd love to do and cannot decide which one to pick, choose the bolder. Choose the path that takes more courage.

- Chances are that a career opportunity will present itself and make your decision easier.

If your interests keep changing

In many respects, college is one big shopping center of interests. You may find yourself inspired by a new subject every week. It's OK to change your interests. Just don't ever treat your interests as trivial. Become good at knowing what you are currently interested in the most.

Still not sure what interests you

Some people struggle for a long time to come to a strong sense of what interests them. If it seems impossible to figure out what your interests are, go about your obligations and your interests and talents will reveal themselves. In the words of Goethe, "How can we learn to know ourselves? Never by reflection but by action. Try to do your duty and you will soon find out what you are. But what is your duty? The demands of the day."

Consider the story of Karen Socher, who graduated from UCLA. Karen remembers her confusion in college.

I spent a lot of time in the library looking for what I was supposed to be doing. I used to walk around the campus reading all the flyers looking for something that would grab my interest. I saw so many things that were interesting, but because of my basic insecurity I'd think, "I can't do that— it's beyond my abilities." On top of that I was lazy and wouldn't try things or give them a chance. I felt trapped in a rut where I wanted to do everything but I wasn't willing

▶ **HOT TIP**

For more help on discovering what would really motivate you, get the workbook *Finding Your Purpose: A Guide to Personal Fulfillment* by Barbara J. Braham. $10.95 through Crisp Publications, www.crisp-pub.com

I never spoke to any of my teachers. I was afraid to— intimidated, shy. I felt like I wouldn't measure up to whatever you're supposed to be as a student. I'd do it different [today] because on my resume, references would be valuable.

Karen Socher, president of Graphic Sound Records

▶ **HOT TIP**

I Could Do Anything If I Only Knew What it Was by Barbara Sher with Barbara Smith (Doubleday).

I was going to be a lawyer because that's what my brother was. But I worked in a law office and I hated it.

Karen Socher

to do anything to get there. There was no solution. I was miserable not knowing what I was going to do with my life. Everybody knew what they wanted to do, but I was just wandering around.

How, in light of her confusion, did she get involved in the music business and become president of the record label Graphic Sound Records, doing work she enjoys very much?

I was on the verge of just giving up. I was working as a legal secretary and getting really depressed. I'd think, "What am I doing with my life? Anything would be better than this!" I got so desperate that I knew I had to do something different. So I took the first opportunity that came along—I volunteered to promote my boyfriend's band to talent agents at a three-day trade show. When the time came to actually go to the trade show, I was terrified. I'd never done anything like that before—put myself in a position where my performance could be judged. But I went through with it and I found that not only was I good at it, but people liked me. It was OK to be myself.

What was the single most important thing that she learned from all this?

You have to do footwork on everything. You have to take enough steps to get to a level where you can decide whether or not the activity is for you. Because otherwise you'll never know. If you're afraid and insecure at the get-go, you're going to assume that you don't like it without even trying it—without giving it a chance. And that's what I used to do. The trade show was a major breakthrough in my life. I was young, I was a woman, and I was enjoying some success at this big event. All of a sudden I felt like I became a special person. People gave me attention and I loved it! I walked away feeling like I could do anything.

Karen broke the cycle of indecision by grabbing onto an opportunity—despite the fact that she felt it was a risky one—and by doing the footwork necessary to experience a measure of personal fulfillment and success. Next you're going to learn something super helpful for college, how to choose the perfect major.

Don't feel guilty if you don't know what you want to do with your life. The most interesting people I know didn't know at 22 what they wanted to do with their lives. . . . Some of the most interesting 40-year-olds I know still don't.

Mary Schmich, Don't Forget to Wear Sunscreen

I never finished anything. For instance, I took dance classes but I quit them before I achieved any level of expertise. But I've decided that my music career is going to be one of the things that I'm going to follow through on so that I will be regarded as a specialist.

Karen Socher

I feel I'm successful mostly because I've become this person who wants to learn and grow—I think that's going to set me apart from the rest. I'm open-minded—totally looking at things around me to see how I can be better or how my business can be better—and I wasn't like that in school.

Karen Socher

CHAPTER 3

Major Excitement

Everybody said, "Don't major in psychology;
you won't be able to find a job where you
can use it." Well, I did. I use it to get people
to jump off a 40-foot crane.

Ron Sherwood,
employee of a bungee-jumping company

The ideal major is the one that you're the most passionate about. Colleges often overemphasize the importance of picking the "right" major, making choosing a major seem like a major life decision—right up there with choosing who you want to spend the rest of your life with. While choosing your major *can* feel like a very big deal, it doesn't have as large an impact on your career as you may think.

For instance, Sue Coleman majored in behavioral pharmacology and now she manages mutual funds. Richard Thau majored in history and now he works in politics. Karen Socher majored in political science and now she works in the music industry. Margot Franssen was a philosophy major and now she owns the international business The Body Shop. Darren Star was an English major and later he went on to create hit television shows like *Melrose Place.* Let me spell it out: YOUR CHOICE OF MAJOR DOESN'T DICTATE WHAT CAREERS YOU'LL BE ABLE TO ENJOY.

First of all, choosing a major is not a life choice. If statistical averages and present-day trends are any indication of how things will go for you, there's a 70% chance your first job will be related to your major. But after that, it's likely that your career will progress like a pinball. Many, if not most people, end up in all kinds of jobs that have nothing to do with their major. Let me put it this way—after your first job, your major

People can expect to change jobs 4.5 times during their 20's.
Bureau of Labor Statistics 1998

When I told my father I was going to be an actor, he said, "Fine, but study welding just in case."
Robin Williams, actor

▶ **HOT TIP**

Most graduates testify that if they had it to do over, they would major in whatever interested them the most.

▶ **HOT TIP**

No matter what you major in, if you can't answer the phone, make a presentation, do a spreadsheet, or write a business letter, nobody needs you.

▶ **HOT TIP**

You can choose a major that is "more likely" to get you a job at graduation, but oftentimes you won't like that job and you'll wish you'd just majored in what interested you.

Students ought to study anything that gets their creative juices flowing—definitely not something that only relates to getting a job. The most useful course I took was a humanitarian course on love.

Margot Franssen, 41, President,
The Body Shop Canada,
philosophy major at York University

becomes about as important as the classes you took in eighth grade, so you can knock "selecting a major" out of the Major Life Decisions category.

Second, selecting your major is not a rags or riches choice because employers aren't looking at your resume to see what you majored in, they're looking to see if you have the basic, practical skill to:

- answer the phone professionally

- write a business letter

- use a computer

- understand marketing

- manage your time effectively

- dress appropriately

If you don't have the skills to do the above, no business needs you—you might as well have drawn yourself a Monopoly card that says "Go directly to the unemployment line. Do not pass go. Do not collect $200." If you do have these skills, you can major in whatever you want. Prove that you have these skills by taking the classes specifically recommended in the chapter entitled "Classes Worth Their Weight in Gold" and/or by getting work experience at a job or internship.

Seriously, if you want to design a special major all about European history, go for it. Employers will hire a European history major as long as s/he has also taken some classes and participated in extracurricular activities that demonstrate a competence in the tasks above (99% of employers are going to require that you've completed an internship, taken business-writing classes, computer classes, and speech classes, etc.). Why would you major in something like European history? Because if European history is your passion, by focusing on it in college you'll enjoy your schooling more and you'll increase your chances of ending up in a career that you absolutely love.

When someone says, "I don't know what really interests me," usually what they're really saying is "My favorite things don't make for a good career." Wrong! There are many careers for every interest you have. So if that's what's holding you back from admitting what really interests you, do a clear and reset. In the next part of the book you'll learn exactly how to link your interests and major to a real-world career that you can get excited about.

CHAPTER 4

No McJobs!

Follow your bliss and be what you want to be.
Don't climb the ladder of success only to
find it's leaning against the wrong wall.

Bernie Siegel, psychologist and writer

If you think that your interests just aren't practical enough,
read the following stories about people whose true interests were as "impractical" as road tripping, reading science
fiction, exercising, playing video games, and beer.

Michael Lane loved most of all to go on road trips so he and
friend James Crotty launched a magazine called *Monk* which
they publish from their RV. The content of the magazine is
basically their travelogue. Their circulation is national and it
makes enough money to support their lifestyle.

- There are many job options for a person interested in
  traveling: travel writer, sales representative, landscape
  photographer, pilot, etc.

Rick Sternbach loved model rockets and science fiction when
he was young and got a job designing the ships and gadgets
you see on *Star Trek: The Next Generation.* He was also able to
apply his interests to a previous job as a science fiction illus-
trator for magazines and books.

- There are many job options for a person with an interest in science fiction and rockets: science fiction writer,
  computer graphics designer, rocket scientist, etc.

Lisa Miller played volleyball for four years during college. She
loved to exercise and stay healthy, so she took that interest

You don't have to be an intellectual.
You don't have to be a scientist. Just
use your natural gifts. You've got
natural gifts. Yeh.
Lyrics from "Natural Gifts"
by The Kinks

If you wanna sing out, sing out. If
you wanna be free, be free. Cause
there's a million ways to be, you
know that there are.
Lyrics from "If You Want to Sing Out,
Sing Out" by Cat Stevens

and established herself as fitness director of a large fitness center.

- There are many job options for a person interested in fitness: nutritionist, wellness teacher, professional bodybuilder, experiential education trainer, personal trainer, etc.

James Robertson has probably tasted more beers from more breweries than anyone. It's "his hobby." In every book he's written, six at last count, he's taken you on a tasting tour describing every beer he's ever tasted. Right now he's tasted over 10,000 beers. One of his books, *The Beer Log*, is over six hundred pages and organized by continent and country. Robertson turned his interest in beer into a career as an author.

- There are many job options for a person interested in beer: author, magazine editor, brewmaster, distributor, marketer, even the entrepreneurial owner of a brew-your-own beer bar.

Chris Lindquist loved to play video games and after college he got a job as a game reviewer for *Electronic Entertainment* magazine.

- There are many job options for a person interested in video games: game tester, game designer, game programmer, arcade owner, virtual reality ride designer, etc.

Any and every interest can be turned into a successful career. If you can't think of jobs that would suit your interests or major, it's probably because of one of the following reasons:

1. You haven't consulted the ULTRA-INCREDIBLE series of career books put out by VGM publishing. Do this: Go to an on-line bookstore and search for "vgm." You'll get a list of over 400 incredibly specific career books like:

   Careers for Night Owls & Other Insomniacs
   Sports Nuts & Other Athletic Types
   Music Lovers & Other Tuneful Types
   Mystery Buffs & Other Snoops and Sleuths
   Travel Buffs & Other Restless Types
   Born Leaders & Other Decisive Types

▶ **HOT TIP**

Check out the book *Nice Job, The Guide to Cool, Odd, Risky, and Gruesome Ways to Make a Living* (Ten Speed Press). It has 84 job listings that tell you everything you need to know.

Cybersurfers & Other Online Types
Good Samaritans and Other Humanitarian Types
Opportunities in Animal & Pet Care Careers
Overseas Careers
Commercial Art and Graphic Design Careers
Cable Television Careers
Nonprofit Organization Careers
Performing Arts Careers
Visual Arts Careers
Beauty Culture Careers

Find the VGM book of your dreams and get it! Maybe it's at your library or career center.

2. You need to ask more people about possible careers.

3. You need to know more about the MILLIONS of career possibilities that there are.

4. You're onto a job that a select few people go into and you'll probably enjoy a unique and interesting career.

I suggest you start by going to your career center or library and looking for *Job Hunter's Sourcebook: Where to Find Employment Leads and Other Job Search Resources* by Michelle Le Compte, editor. If you don't find this book, ask a staff person to help you find something similar.

Ask as many people as you can what careers are related to your interest. Ask enough people and someone's going to suggest a great job that you never knew existed! A word of caution: Many people you ask will discourage you with statements like, "No such job exists," "It's not possible," or "I wouldn't recommend it." Thank them for their input and move on to asking the next person. You're on a mission and you're going to have to pass a lot of people with limited vision and personal fears.

Try the job idea generator . . .

You can also get a real-world idea of possible careers by running your idea through something I developed called the JOB IDEA GENERATOR. It gives you a picture of the jobs that are possible for you. It may not give you the job specifics, but once you know the kind of work that is possible, you can easily look up the job title and company address on your own.

To waste any time doing something you don't really love is, to me, the ultimate waste of time.

Peter Jennings

▶ **HOT TIP**

The Art Job Web site lists job opportunities in the arts. www.artjob.org

▶ **HOT TIP**

TCG's Art Search is a newsletter published twice a month about job opportunities in the theater and arts. $54/yr.

Here's how it works. Simply take what really interests you and ask yourself these questions:

- How could I be paid to inform people about this interest? (Perhaps through writing, consulting, speaking, TV, newsletters, magazines, shows, lectures, books, or computer bulletin boards.)

- How could I be paid to provide other people with a service related to this interest?

- How could I be paid to perform this interest for other people?

- How could I be paid to create products related to this interest?

- How could I be paid to assist people who are focused on this interest?

- How could I be paid to learn more about this interest?

If you did the JOB IDEA GENERATOR you might be ready to call the career center or other knowledgeable professionals and ask them to help you with the specific job title/job description/salary range or the kinds of work that you identified as attractive. Or you can go straight to an INCREDIBLE book: *Professional Careers Sourcebook: Where to Find Help Planning Careers That Require College or Technical Degrees*, edited by Kathleen M. Savage and Annette Novallo (Gale, 1993). This book has everything you need to discover and learn about 118 professions. For each profession it lists multiple career guidebooks, professional associations, test guides, educational programs, handbooks, newsletters, professional meetings, and even annual conventions. This book makes figuring out where to get important how-to information about your career so easy to find that you might as well be taking cuts to the front of the line. I love this book! (Another book that is quite good is *The Encyclopedia of Second Careers* by Gene R. Hawes. It contains career descriptions, association phone numbers, salaries, and skill requirements for over 200 careers.)

Need some more ideas? Try the SUPER-SIMPLE, UNIQUE & WEIRD JOB IDEA JOGGER! It couldn't be simpler. Fill in the blanks of the following sentence:

A great job would be [verb] in the [your interest] field.

> A person should go into their job because they love it—not to be famous—if fame is all they want, they're going to have a miserable time.
>
> *Julia Stiles*

> I had an uncle who used to constantly ask me, "Why don't you get a real job?" People always thought I was jerking around, and quite frankly, I wasn't making any money at it, so I'd even think, "What am I doing with my career?"
>
> *Howard Stern*

For example, if you're interested in astronomy and you like to read you get the sentence:

A great job would be reading in the astronomy field.

Reading in the astronomy field? What jobs does that make your think of? Hmmmm . . . Editor of an astronomy magazine? Researcher for NASA? Author of books about the latest astronomy developments?

Now change the verb to drawing and see what happens:

A great job would be drawing in the astronomy field.

What ideas does that jog? Hmmmm . . . Illustrating astronomy books? Architecturally designing observatories? Mapping star systems? Science fiction paintings?

Try this technique out with your own interests and choice of verbs. You might be surprised at the unique and weird job ideas it jogs in your mind.

Enjoy yourself as much as possible

A lot of people might suggest that you choose a career based on your strongest talents. I caution you about choosing a career by asking the question "What am I best at?" You may happen to be good at something you don't necessarily enjoy. I'm really good at running, parallel parking, and typing. But I wouldn't enjoy being a marathon runner, a valet parking attendant, or an administrative assistant. I have no dreams about any of those careers. Start from what activities you'd enjoy doing regularly and go get the skills required.

People will also encourage you to choose a boring, ordinary, safe job because they don't want you to fail. But remember this: Failure is a lot more likely when you're trying for a career that you don't enjoy. Picture this: Two people working side by side, one from obligation and one from enthusiasm. Which one do you think is most likely to succeed? And which one do you think is most likely to stagnate, get passed over for promotions, dislike the job, and feel like a failure?

Somehow, college makes it seem like you should only aim for a career that fits into the category of Very Serious & Practical Work. That's fine if at heart you are a serious and practical person. But if deep down inside, you are very serious about having fun, don't let college erase your memory of all the jobs that fall into the category of Very Seriously Fun Work. Just in case you can't think of many fun jobs, check out

The universe does not send us a telegram saying, "Do this, take that job; that's your soul mate." The universe is more subtle than that. Simply notice what comes your way. If something comes up and it strikes a chord, put it in your back pocket and just let it be. Should it come up a second time, take it out and examine it, then set the idea someplace within easy reach, but still don't do anything about it. When it comes up a third time, LISTEN. The universe is talking to you.
Deborah Nuckols, student, quoted in Thinking about Thinking *by Clark McKowen*

My mother always encouraged me to pursue my work and I don't think she's ever said, "Why aren't you married?" Or, "Hurry up, you're past thirty." She's always been far more interested in creative pursuits than maternal and marital ones. And by doing that she's cleared away a huge obstacle that I think a lot of other women face.

Susan Faludi, writer

the list of over 60-plus unusual jobs that I've included in the Going Pro chapter.

And also remember that college isn't necessarily for getting an intellectual career. It isn't necessarily for getting a high-paying career. College is for developing your talents so that you can learn and do anything you like. When you start to focus on what you like, life starts to get really great.

If you want a really rare, unusual job

A lot of students dream of a getting a really cool, unusual, quirky, or high-profile job, but are hesitant to pursue it because the career path is narrow and undefined. Remember: The narrow path is more fun, it is more adventurous, and it is more rewarding. You were not meant to settle for a normal and safe job. You were meant to express yourself in a unique, exciting, cool way. You were meant to make your mark. You have urges and dreams about unique, exciting, cool jobs. Your destiny is speaking to you through those urges.

You can be the next one who makes it big but you have to practice, read, study, and learn. You have to commit to developing your raw talent into mastery. You have to be the first to recognize your star potential, and then be the driving force behind the development of your mastery. Your raw talent will turn into mastery if you polish your skills with persistence and passion. It is the only way anyone has ever "made it." For instance, a professional comedy writer is an amateur who didn't give up.

There are many myths about jobs on the less traveled narrow path: There's no guidance. You're likely to starve. The coolest jobs are one in a million. They require great talent. Simply put, these are all myths, lies and *bulls@$t* passed around by people who are letting their fears get the best of them. Jobs on the narrow and less traveled path are: exciting and cool, envy inducing, big time rewarding and AVAILABLE for the brave of heart, so go for it. Read on because your life gets even greater when you follow your heart and let money follow you....

People can call me [a] madman, but when you think about it, the rest of the world lives in a box, gets into another box, drives off to work, then spends the whole day looking into another box. To me, that's masochistic.

Matt Parry—traveling across America on a push scooter to benefit the homeless

Regret for the things we did can be tempered by time; it is regret for the things we did not do that is inconsolable.

Sydney J. Harris, writer

I learned never to give up from my dad. He taught me it's better to go after something special and risk starving to death than to surrender. If you give up your dream, what's left?

Jim Carrey

Do not follow where the path may lead. Go instead where there is no path and leave a trail.

Ralph Waldo Emerson

CHAPTER 5

Money Matters

Being rich isn't about money. Being rich is a state of mind. Some of us, no matter how much money we have, will never be free enough to take time to stop and eat the heart of the watermelon. And some of us will be rich without ever being more than a paycheck ahead of the game.

Harvey B. Mackay,
Entrepreneur and Author

A Letter Home from College

Dear Dad,

$chool i$ really great. I am making lot$ of friend$ and $tudying very hard. With all my $tuff, I $imply can't think of anything I need, $o if you would like, you can ju$t $end me a card, a$ I would love to hear from you.

Love,

Your $on

Do what you love and the necessary money will follow. The necessary resources will follow. What will not appear is all the money that would be nice and make everything rosey.
Peter McWilliams and John Roger

Dear Son,

I kNOw that astroNOmy, ecoNOmics, and oceaNOgraphy are eNOugh to keep even an hoNOr student busy. Do NOt forget that the pursuit of kNOwledge is a NOble task, and you can never study eNOugh.

Love,

Dad

Money is an article which may be used as a universal passport to everywhere except heaven, and as a universal provider for everything except happiness.
Wall Street Journal

Be true to your heart

Do you identify with a job that doesn't seem to pay much? Remember the words of Joseph Campbell, "Follow your bliss. There's something inside of you that knows when you're on the beam or off the beam. And if you get off the beam to earn money, you've lost your life. And if you stay in the center and don't get money, you still have your bliss."

Many people, including myself, have found that the best way to pick a job is by the amount of ENJOYMENT, SATISFACTION, and LEARNING that the job has to offer. Consider the true-life story of Joy Greenidge, a field director for PLAN, a nonprofit that helps destitute children. Joy took a low-paying job with the agency and has enjoyed her work so much that she's passed up opportunities to move up in her organization where she would get paid more. What is her reward since it's not monetary? "In this job, no day is the same as any other," she says. "What can I say? It's been a wonderful life."

Jimmy Buffett, who's a celebrity musician, a *New York Times* best-selling author, and the founder of a successful restaurant chain called Margaritaville, was asked how he made so many successful decisions. He replied, "I remove money from the consideration. I ask myself, 'If money wasn't part of the decision would I do it?' If it sounds appealing without money, then I go for it." A lot of people turn their backs on the career of their dreams because they think that a low salary will make them unhappy. But beyond not being able to make a living, money has very little to do with happiness. Consider Jim Carrey's story. He was making several hundred thousand dollars a year as an impressionist when he reached a point where he really wanted to be recognized for having unique comedic talents. So much so that he quit doing impressions and walked away from an extraordinary income. His friends said, "You're insane. Don't do this." Jim said, "If it doesn't make me happy, what the f—k good is it? I'll have a lot of money and feel like an idiot."

Artists are often pursuing careers that are out of the mainstream and require an uncommon amount of sacrifice and risk. If this is you, by all means continue reading this book because its recommendations were written with you in mind. But because the arts are primarily not given their deserved legitimacy and proper place in our society the

You must get money to chase you, but never let it catch up.
Denis Waitley

Why is there so much month left at the end of the money?
John Barrymore

Money, it turned out, was exactly like sex, you thought of nothing else if you didn't have it and thought of other things if you did.
James Baldwin

Our income is like our shoes; if too small, they gall and pinch us; but if too large, they cause us to stumble and trip.
C. C. Colton

following excerpt is exclusively for you. It comes from the book *The Gift of Giving* by Michael Lynberg.

> *In your heart you may wish to be a painter, an actor, a writer, or a musician. You may be willing to give your life for your art, to sacrifice everything for creative excellence, beauty, and truth. This sacrifice may be necessary, for the life of the artist, while full of adventure and the thrill of creativity and discovery, can also be lonely and without the rewards valued by much of society. "Perhaps it will turn out that you are called to be an artist," wrote Ranier Maria Rilke in his* Letters to a Young Poet. *Then take that destiny upon yourself and bear it, its burden and its greatness, without asking what recompense might come from the outside. For the creator must be a world for himself.*

Finally, a word for that part in us that can be determined to make good money. The chart below is to give you some proof that just about any job you're passionate about, no matter how odd, cool, or quirky, has awesome earning potential. If money matters to you, never forget that doctors, lawyers, and engineers aren't the only ones raking in the cash. You can follow your passion and make bank. (P.S.—The real average salary of a doctor is $64,000; for lawyers it's around $75,000. Good money, but then again, some rodeo clowns are making $90,000.)

Money is better than poverty, if only for financial reasons.
Woody Allen

You should be looking for the joy, the struggle, and the challenge of work. What you bring forth from your own guts and heart. The happiness of hard work. No amount of money can buy that. Those are the things of the spirit.
Jacob Needleman

The Mind-Expanding, Options-Enhancing, Eye Poppin' Chart of OTHER Jobs That Make Big Bank

Airport manager	$130,000
Animation and digital effects background layout	$91,000
Animation and digital effects staff writer	$175,500
Antiques dealer	$50,000
Art dealer	$175,000
Art museum curator	$65,000
Athletic footwear designer	$130,000
Book publishing professional	$44,000
Brewmaster	$80,000
Camera operator	$46,300
Canoe instructor and coach	$45,000
CEO of a nonprofit organization	$100,000
Character animator	$106,900
Clergy, Priest, Rabbi, or Minister	$62,000

Money is good, but money shouldn't buy us.
Adamu Lamu

Money isn't everything, but it ranks right up there with oxygen.
Rita Davenport

Clothing/jewelry/cosmetics generalist	$41,000
Comedy writer	$80,000
Commercial airline pilot	$200,000
Computer game designer	$78,000
Demolition contractor	$100,000
Diamond cutter	$150,000
Director of volunteers at a nonprofit organization	$84,000
Disc jockey	$40,000
Dog walker (in New York City)	$50,000
Environmentalist	$65,000
Executive chef	$75,000
Fashion designer	$50,000
FBI agent	$52,400
Film director	$160,200
Film editor	$70,000
Fire and crash rescue	$48,000
Fire fighter	$50,000
Flight safety inspector	$85,000
Foreign diplomat	$54,500
Forest products technologist	$58,680
Forestry researcher	$70,000
Fundraiser	$46,500
Geologist	$50,000
Golf sales representative	$130,000
Graphic designer	$45,000*
Hazardous waste manager	$51,000
Helicopter pilot	$72,500
Hypnotherapist	$60,000
Interior designer	$60,000
Internet strategist	$115,000
Inventor	$90,000
Landscape architect	$53,900
Librarian	$54,600
Library director	$58,200
Lifeguard	$52,000
Lobbyist	$80,000
Magazine editor	$65,000
Magician (on a cruise ship)	$100,000
Massage therapist	$50,000
Midwife	$55,000

When I chased after money, I never had enough. When I got my life on purpose and focused on giving of myself and everything that arrived into my life, then I was prosperous.

Wayne Dyer

I don't want to make money. I just want to be wonderful.

Marilyn Monroe

Money is like manure. If you spread it around it does a lot of good. But if you pile it up in one place it stinks like hell.

Jr. Murchison

Motion picture art director	$115,000
Music talent scout	$80,000
Newspaper editor	$60,000
Organic farmer	$50,000
Philosopher	$60,000
Photo editor (at a magazine)	$60,000
Political campaign worker	$60,000
Politician	$90,000
Portrait photographer	$49,200
Private investigator	$60,000
Product name developer	$100,000
Radio news director	$102,676
Recreation specialist—aquatics	$40,000
Reptile keeper at a zoo (herpetologist)	$40,000
Restaurant critic	$75,000
Rock concert promoter	$48,000
Rodeo clown	$90,000
Senior high school principal	$66,600
Sky diving instructor	$42,000
Sports manager	$44,000
Stage technician	$45,000
Syndicated cartoonist	$100,000
Talent agent	$41,000
Toy designer	$58,000
Translator	$35,000
Travel writer	$72,000
TV news anchor	$200,000
TV news photographer	$120,000
TV reporter	$79,637
TV sportscaster	$128,877
TV weathercaster	$150,000
Wedding consultant	$75,000
Zoo director	$90,000

*Graphic designer is a prime example of the severe limits of this chart. I personally know designers who make six-figure incomes. Remember, your income can exceed what we've listed in this chart.

Sources: You name it, we pulled from it. We researched magazines, trade journals, institutes, surveys, and Web pages. (We did, however, steer clear of using any writing on bathroom walls.)

I know of nothing more despicable and pathetic than a man who devotes all the hours of the waking day to the making of money for money's sake.
John D. Rockefeller

It doesn't matter how rich or how poor you are, you can still afford to do the little, magical, ordinary things that make life great.
R.C. Dini, author of How to Outlive and Out Do Every One

Don't let your mind dwell on money at all, if you can help it. Throw yourself, body, soul, and spirit into whatever you are doing.
Harry Thayer

Money doesn't worry me. All I care about is a good blue suit. . . . It doesn't even have to be good.
Will Rogers

You may think to yourself, "Hey, these are much higher than the average starting salaries people have been showing me for my major. What's up with that?" Remember, it's not where you start—it's where you can end up! Starting salaries go up before long to numbers like those on the previous chart.

Money, money, money!

It's not a bad idea to look to those who've made a lot of money for advice and perspective. About money, Madonna said, "Money's not important. I never think I want to make millions and millions of dollars but I don't want to have to worry about it. The more money you have the more problems you have. I went from making no money to making comparatively a lot and all I've had is problems. Life was simpler when I had no money, when I just barely survived." Jerry Seinfeld said, "I don't really care about the money. In my business, the only way you get as much money as I have is if you don't care about money and you care about comedy; then you end up with money. I'm not the kind of person who could do a show and think, 'Well, we've kind of run out of gas here, but the money's great and the ratings are still good, so let's keep grinding them out.' That would break my heart."

A quick story to end the chapter. There once was a wise Zen monk who lived deep in the woods. People traveled from far and wide to see him. He refused no one. One day a young reporter decided to write the story of the wise man, so he paid the monk a visit. The reporter started with this question, "Of all the different people who come to see you, which do you prefer, rich people or poor people?" "Rich people," said the monk without hesitating. This surprised the reporter, who was expecting an evasive Zen answer about everyone being different yet equal. "Why rich people?" "Because," said the monk, "they already know that money won't make them happy."

OK, with a determination to follow your heart into a cool, unique, and rewarding job you're ready for the best step yet. The exciting step. The step that makes it all worthwhile. The light at the end of the tunnel.

If I ever get real rich, I hope I'm not real mean to poor people, like I am now.

Jack Handey

Don't judge yourself by somebody else's standards. You will always lose.

Billy Corgan of the Smashing Pumpkins

Work like you don't need money, love like you've never been hurt, and dance like no one's watching.

Lyrics by U2

CHAPTER 6

Your Ultimate Life

Greatness is a measure in one's spirit, not in
the results of one's rank in human affairs.

Sherman Finesilver

As a kid, Conan O'Brien sat around the dinner table
entertaining his family with jokes. He grew up and created a life for himself entertaining a national audience every
night. Jane Goodall dreamed of living in Africa and writing
about animals ever since she saw *Dr. Doolittle* at age eight. Jay
Leno's two loves during his teens were cars and comedy—not
only does he now do comedy every evening but he also has a
large college of exotic automobiles. As a kid John Singleton
watched movies on a 70-foot drive-in movie screen outside his
window and dreamed of being a moviemaker—now he's an
established A-list director in Hollywood.

The testimonials that following your passion leads you to
your dream life go on and on. Modern dance legend Martha
Graham said, "My fate was sealed," referring to the night
when she was seventeen and saw an incredible dance performance. Robin Williams described the year in college that he
flunked out of political science but discovered improvisa-
tional theater. "Everything opened up, the whole world just
changed in that one year." Oprah Winfrey hosted a talk show
and liked it so much she said, "This is what I should be doing.
It's like breathing." When discussing his success, David
Letterman said, "All I ever wanted was to have my own television show." Michael Stipe, lead singer of R.E.M., said, "I
heard Patti Smith's album *Horses* and it gave me, you know…
it gave me strength, it gave me incredible strength, and I
knew immediately that that's what I wanted to do."

Keep away from people who try to
belittle your ambitions. Small
people always do that, but the
really great make you feel that you,
too, can become great.

Mark Twain

If you get up and asked how you
could use your life to help others,
your life would truly change.

Oprah Winfrey

You gotta live life for yourself
You can't live life for anyone else
You gotta live life that's all you do
Nobody gonna live your life for you
Lyrics from "Live Life" by The Kinks

What if these people had decided to pursue something more "practical" or more "realistic"? Life is very generous to those who follow their passions and pursue their dreams.

We all have a destiny and it speaks to us through our passions and dreams. When you have clarity about what you really want out of life, it's easier to choose jobs you'll excel at and love. You can bring your passions and dreams front and center with a tool that is 99 percent effective, totally valuable, and unimaginably powerful: power journalizing. Apply pen to paper, or keys to keyboard, and answer questions such as:

- What am I excited about in my life right now?

- What am I most grateful about in my life now?

- What is it I have not yet done, that I truly desire to do before I die?

- What action could I take today that would lead me to my dream life?

- What would I want for myself if I knew I could have it any way I wanted?

Why journalizing is so powerful

Power journalizing gives you the opportunity to answer powerful questions. Answering powerful questions gives you powerful answers. For instance, most students go through college constantly asking themselves, "How can I get better grades?" At best, this question will encourage your mind to come up with more ways to get A's. A more powerful question you could journalize about is, "What would I do if I knew I couldn't fail?" This question will produce answers about your dreams, aspirations, passions, and goals.

I got an email from a recent graduate telling me she had done all the things this book suggests yet still didn't know what to do with her life. She was desperate for help. I told her I could help if she would email me some entries from her journal. She emailed back, "I don't journalize. That's one thing from your book I didn't do." I wasn't surprised by her answer.

I've journalized since I was 19 and it's been an incredible help. Journalizing gives you clarity. In the book *Think and Grow Rich* by Napoleon Hill, the author challenges you to ask

Show me whom you envy and I'll show you whom you ache to become. In determining what job a person would kill for, for instance, envy is far more accurate than any survey, horoscope, or aptitude test.

M. G. Lord, writer

I live a life of curiosity and I get paid for it.

Larry King, talk show host

I vowed to apply my inventory of experiences to the solving of problems that affect everyone aboard planet Earth.

R. Buckminster Fuller

Here's to the future! The only limits are the limits of your imagination. Dream up the world you want to live in, dream out loud, in high volume.

Lyrics by U2

the first hundred people you meet what they want most in life. Hill says, "Ninety-eight of them will not be able to tell you. If you press them for an answer, some will say *security;* many will say *money;* a few will say *happiness;* others will say *fame and power;* and still others will say *social recognition, ease in living, ability to sing, dance, or write;* but none of them will be able to define these terms or give the slightest indication of a plan by which they hope to attain these vaguely expressed wishes. Riches do not respond to wishes. They respond only to definite plans, backed by definite desires, through constant persistence."

When you journalize, you quickly become a two per-center who can clearly define what you want, name your definite plan, and be certain about your definite desire.

More questions to journalize about

- What are the most important things in your life?

- What are the activities that you love and enjoy most today?

- What would be your ideal work environment today?

- How would your ideal work day go today?

- How would you define success today?

- What might be your purpose or destiny?

- How do you want to be perceived by your friends? Co-workers? Parents? Significant other?

- What magazine would you most like to be featured in for your tremendous accomplishments in 10 years?

- What would you like to be the best in the world at?

- Who are your heroes and what is it about them that you most want to be like?

- What do you really really think should be changed in the world?

- What do you most want to be remembered for at the end of your life?

- Whom do you envy and what is it about them that you envy?

Life is only what you make of it
So make the verses rhyme and all the pieces fit
There isn't any time to make much sense of it
It soon fades away
Lyrics from "Moving Pictures" by The Kinks

And you can dream
So dream out loud
And don't let the bastards grind you down
Lyrics by U2

Your imagination is a preview to life's coming attractions.
Albert Einstein

Life's most urgent question is, what are you doing for others?
Martin Luther King, Jr.

Know thy values

Also journalize about your values. Look in the side margin at the list of workplace values and choose the five that you want most from a job. Base your answer on past experiences or simply on the way you feel today. Then prioritize your five choices, one being the most important value to you, five being the fifth most important. It's been said that if you **don't** know what you value most you'll fall for anything. Meaning, you'll fall for a crap job.

The great thing about knowing your top five **values** is you'll be able to decide whether a job is for you or **not**. It goes like this: If a job is only going to satisfy one of your top five values, every day on that job you'd probably find yourself thinking, "This job sucks!" If you get a job that meets two out of five, then it would probably be, "My job's OK, but I'd like to find something better." Three out of five and you'll be thinking, "I've got a pretty good job." Four out of five and it's, "My job is awesome!" And when you hone in on a job that satisfies all five of your top five values, you'll be one of the fortunate few who can say, "I've got my dream job! I can't believe they pay me to do it!"

Tips on journalizing

For starters, in a diary you mostly reflect on how your day went. In journalizing you mostly write about how you desire your ideal days to be. Not, "My day went like this…" Instead, "Ideally my days will be like this…"

Also,

- Continually revise.

- Write when you're inspired.

- Write when you're reflective.

- Write when you don't want to make the same mistake ever again.

- Think big.

- Write from the heart.

- Write more from the heart than from the head.

- Work it, work it, work it—turn a one-paragraph answer into a page.

- Spell out your dreams specifically, right down to the smallest details about what you want.

- Describe your dreams accomplished in the most successful manner possible.

- Don't use the phrases "I want" or "I desire" or "I wish" or "I hope." There is only "I am" and "I will be."

Ultimately there is no right or wrong way to journalize. There is only the act of clarifying your ideal life, defining your unique self, and—very important—having faith that it will all come true.

When I first started journalizing I was hard pressed to come up with answers longer than a few sentences. But once I started, there was no turning back. My mind was engaged and I began getting floods of answers at the oddest times. (Apparently my subconscious mind and heart were anxious to finally be heard.) I'd wake up in the middle of the night remembering an ambition I had almost totally forgotten. An incredible detail to my ideal workday would suddenly come to me while eating lunch. A phrase or quote a friend or professor said would send me running to journalize. It's a process like this that transforms you from a person with loosely based wishes and dreams into a person with high motivation, passion, and a plan. It is a process like this that enables you to define who you truly are.

The weird, unexplainable thing about journalizing

There is an even more awesome benefit to journalizing, but it is discussed less often because it can come across like an episode of the *X-Files*. Journalizing creates your reality. What you journalize about comes true quicker and often in seemingly strange and coincidental ways. On many occasions I have journalized one day about something I desired to come true, only to "coincidentally" meet the right person, discover the perfect resource, or get the perfect lucky break the very next day. One explanation for this lies in the truth that you must know what you want. Your unconscious mind has genius power to filter for, direct you to, and even attract things and resources that will help you create what you have said you want. Journalizing makes you very clear on what you want and allows your subconscious to go to work.

> The answer will hit, like a big psychic orgasm, if you listen to your dreams. They never lie.
> *E. Jean Carroll*

> Did you ever try to pick a cold medicine? You stand there going, "Well, this one is quick acting, but this one is long lasting..." Which is more important, the present or the future?
> *Jerry Seinfeld*

> If you want something bad enough, the whole earth conspires to help you get it.
> *Madonna*

UNABLE TO ANSWER QUESTION 23, "WHAT PERSONAL GOALS DO YOU HAVE TO GIVE YOUR OWN LIFE MEANING," FENTON PEEKS AT HIS NEIGHBOR'S PAPER.

Build a dream and the dream will build you.

Robert Schuller

Everyone who has taken a shower has had ideas. It's the person who gets out of that shower and does something with that idea who makes the difference.

Nolan Bushwell

The mind is the limit. As long as the mind can envision the fact that you can do something, you can do it as long as you really believe 100 percent.

Arnold Schwarzenegger

Harvard Business School did an interesting study. They found that 3 percent of the American population had specific goals written down. Ten percent had specific goals, but not written down. Sixty percent had vague goals. And sadly, a full 27 percent of the population did not know the difference between a goal and wish. (A wish is a statement like, "I'd love to get a great job." A goal is "I'm going to get a great job." It's the difference between believing you have control over your destiny or not.) The surprise of the study was that of the 13 percent who had specific goals, the first 3 percent who had them written down were more than ten times more likely to have their dreams come true.

Jim Carrey's story is a classic example of this mysterious power of writing down your dreams. Carrey went to Los Angeles to pursue his dream of being in the movies. He came from Canada and his family was so poor they were actually homeless for a while, but he was determined to make something of himself. One night in 1990 he got in his car and drove to the top of the Hollywood Hills so that he could have a better view of the city. While overlooking the city, he took out his checkbook and wrote HIMSELF a check in the amount of TEN MILLION DOLLARS; he postdated the check for Thanksgiving 1995 (five years later); wrote the words "Acting Services Rendered" in the memo section, signed the check and placed it in his wallet to carry with him. In 1995 he received his first humongous paycheck, a check in the amount of $7 million for his role in the film *Dumb & Dumber.* Later that year he was paid in excess of $10 million for *Batman.* "It wasn't about money. I knew if I was making that much, I'd be working with the best people on the best material. That's always been my dream."

Carrey's story illustrates a very deep truth. Your thoughts are creative. Turning your thoughts into words is even more powerful. Thoughts, words, and actions together are magnificently effective in giving birth to your reality. From the book *Conversations with God,* according to God, "You create everything in your reality. Life will take off for you when you choose for it to. Do you want your life to 'take off'? Begin at once to imagine it the way you want it to be—and move into that."

How journalizing leads you to know what you're truly passionate about

- You'll make better choices about what to get yourself involved in (from classes to jobs to summer experiences) and you'll waste less time on things that don't interest you.

- Journalizing is a very effective way to get your heart talking. When you were a kid you probably listened to your heart more. For instance, in second grade I voluntarily entered a talent show and gave a monologue. Then in high school I stood up in front of all the students and ran the assemblies. Yet in college I forgot how much I liked speaking. It wasn't until age 26 that all my journalizing reminded me that I truly loved speaking.

Every dream is worthy

One person's dream is to save the world, another's is to make a million dollars, and another's is to have a television show. It doesn't matter that their focuses are different because each person has a unique destiny. It's just important that you are tapped into the dream that keeps you energized on the highway of life. (One note of caution for those whose dreams might be all about making money: Studies have shown that the more money a person strives to make, the less likely s/he is to be happy. A healthier alternative might be to dream about achieving mastery of certain skills that happen to make you lots of money.)

When you know your dreams and you know the subjects and work that really interest you, you are in the same starting position as the vast majority of people who go on to greatness. Now you need to get past your FEARS. Fear of competition, failure, lack of money....

I always knew I would do something, and do it right. I believed it. I mean, I really, really believe it. I think you have to if you're going to make it happen.
Tommy Hilfiger

The secret of getting ahead is getting started.
Unknown

You can have it all. You just can't have it all at once.
Oprah Winfrey

▶ **HOT TIP**
Carry a small pocket notebook with you to capture the thoughts you'd like to journalize about.

CHAPTER 7

The Six Big Fears

Pick a time and a place to deal with your
fears or your fears will pick the time and the
place, and they will deal with you.

Duncan Brassington

M ichael Elliot was a student I met after my presentation at
the University of Arkansas. He grew up in a small
Oklahoma town called Dewey. After his sophomore year he
was planning to go back to the same summer job he'd had
the year before, at a restaurant. It paid decent money and it
was very convenient.

Six months after we had met he contacted me again. He
said he'd left my talk thinking a lot about what he really
dreamed of doing in life. It dawned on him that he thought
Matt Damon had the coolest job in the world and he wanted
to work in Hollywood. However, Hollywood was 3,000 miles
away and in a state he'd never been to. As a matter of fact,
he'd never been outside of Oklahoma or Arkansas. To make
matters worse, Michael had never taken any classes in film,
acting, theater, or even creative arts. But instead of assuming
his dream was impossible, he decided to take a chance.

He went to his career center to see if they had any
Hollywood internships. He met with the unfortunate news
that they did not. Instead of giving up there, Michael took
another chance. He went to the library to see if they had any
books that might help him find Hollywood jobs. They did.

Two days later, Michael was reading about Hollywood
jobs when he got a call from the career center. They had
just received an announcement for a summer internship at
Miramax films in Los Angeles. The news sent chills down
Michael's spine. His first thought was filled with fear, "They'd

So many times people end up
fixated on doing things right, that
they end up doing nothing at all.
Wright brothers, aviation pioneers

Two Wrights don't make a
wrong, but they do make a
pretty good airplane.
Anonymous

Love your parents and teachers,
but love your truth the most.
Confucius

never pick me." But then he thought, "I've got a one in a million chance of being the one they pick, but if I don't try, that puts my chances at zero." So Michael sent Miramax his resume and a cover letter.

Let me insert a brief comment here. I've personally met hundreds of students who have extraordinary jobs, and one thing has become quite clear. The people who get the coolest jobs are almost always the people who tried for jobs they figured they couldn't get. *Chances aren't given. They're taken.*

Michael took his chances and it paid off. "Somehow, someway, Miramax films picked me," he told me. "It was the greatest time of my entire life! For instance, I was required—required—to go to all the Miramax premier parties. At one party, for the movie *Friday the 13th,* I found myself taking pictures with the star, Jamie Lee Curtis." He went on, "Plus, I met some students in LA who were interning at Disneyland and before you knew it, so was I! Two dream internships! And then, at the end of the summer, as part of my internship, I went on two free cruises on the new Disney ship!"

I asked Michael, "What was the greatest thing about your summer in Hollywood?" I thought he might answer "meeting the stars," "living in a big city," or "going on the Bahamas cruise," but he surprised me by saying, "Now I understand *it's reachable.*"

Your wildest dreams are reachable, but you must take chances, and taking chances means beating your fear. Had Michael Elliot let his fears stop him from trying for his Hollywood dream, he would have settled instead for a repeat performance at the restaurant in Dewey.

All humans are afraid of something. There are SIX Big Fears in particular that usually stop people from pursuing the job of their dreams:

- Fear of poverty
- Fear of what other people expect
- Fear of competition
- Fear of choosing the wrong thing
- Fear of not having the right experience
- Fear of failure

I didn't have squat when I came to the States. The worst thing that could happen is I could be back where I started—and I was having fun back then.
Michael Bates, CEO and founder of Software Marketing Corp.

You gotta go get it. It's your life go live it. Round the corner give it some gas.
Paul Westerburg, singer/songwriter

Fear of poverty is, without doubt, the most destructive of the six basic fears.
Napoleon Hill,
Think and Grow Rich

There are others, for certain, like fear of not having the right major, fear of moving to a new city, fear of not liking it if it does come true—but naming all the different fears doesn't matter. Stiff competition, parental expectations, wrong credentials, lack of connections, lack of experience, lack of money, lack of talent, etc., never stop a person from reaching their dreams. There is only one thing in the world that stops people from reaching their destiny: Fear. Fear can and will stop you, *if you let it.*

I interviewed the one and only Super Bowl champion, Heisman Trophy–winning, MVP legend, NFL running back Marcus Allen. One question I asked him was, "What does fear mean to a person as accomplished as you?" His eyes lit up and he delivered his words like a fire chief teaching emergency instructions. "You have to collide with fear. You have to attack fear," he said, without flinching. He continued:

> *What I'm about to tell you, I'm more proud of than ANY of my football accomplishments. I've always been afraid of the water. Growing up in San Diego, my buddies were always going to the beach to play in the ocean. I'd always make up an excuse to not go with them, and I never went in the water. Two years ago, when I was thirty-six years old, I decided it was time to attack that fear so I signed up for scuba diving lessons. Talk about facing your fears—I was suddenly sixty feet underwater and being told to keep calm while I shared my respirator with a buddy. Everything on the football field is easy compared to keeping your cool while you're sharing your air sixty feet underwater. But, I attacked my fear and it opened up a whole new world for me. I do everything now: water ski, jet ski, surf, scuba dive. But I never knew all I was missing until I faced my fear. Fear causes you to miss fantastic opportunities.*

And then Marcus Allen sent chills down my spine by saying, "That's the thing about fear. Death will kill you once, but fear kills you over and over and over, if you let it."

Five prescriptions for fear:

1. Feel the fear and do it anyway.

2. Get support from friends who believe in you.

3. Remember, you are equipped to handle anything that comes your way.

The real dividing line is passion. As long as you believe that what you're doing is MEANINGFUL, you can cut through fear and exhaustion and take the next step.

Arlene Blum

Gonna stand my ground, won't be turned around and I'll keep this world from draggin' me down gonna stand my ground and I won't back down
*Lyrics from "I Won't Back Down"
by Tom Petty*

Fear is the only thing that can stop a person from reaching their dreams.
Paulo Coehlo, The Alchemist

4. Know that F.E.A.R. is a False Expectation About Risk.

5. Replace your fear with faith.

Feel the fear and do it anyway

You could call this the Marcus Allen school of thought about fear management. Attack your fears. Push through your fears. Feel the fear and do it anyway. The alternative is to let fear stop you and then have to deal with the regret of not even trying. Jim Carrey has a good story about feeling the fear and doing it anyway. "I've always tried to be somebody special. I used to go up to the Comedy Store to find something new. I promised myself that I wouldn't repeat a word I said the night before. Two-thirds of the time, it was garbage, but sometimes things would come out that were really kinda beautiful, and nice. That's the abyss, you know. You have to go right to the edge."

Get support from friends who believe in you

The Beatles said it well when they sang, "Help! I need somebody. Help! Not just anybody. Help, you know I need someone. Heeeeeelllllllp!" The CEO of Coca Cola was once asked what he thought separated the ones who do OK from the ones who make it to the very top. He answered, "The ones who make it to the top are excellent at asking for help." When you have fears and insecurities about doing something, ask someone who believes in you, "Do you think I've got a chance of pulling this off? Can you offer me any advice for increasing my chances?" This will work wonders for your courage.

Remember, you are equipped to handle anything that comes your way

A fourth grader once said, "You have nothing to fear but homework." Think about it—have you ever *not* been able to handle a situation? When you face scary challenges where you risk failure or humiliation, what you're likely to find is that it's not as tough as you thought it was going to be. You have what it takes to make it through.

Life shrinks or expands in proportion to one's courage.
Anaïs Nin

It is one of the great jokes of existence. Courageously journey to the center of your fear and you'll find nothing—just fear being afraid of itself.
Peter McWilliams and John Rogers

The irony is that the person NOT taking risks feels the same amount of fear. The non-risk taker simply feels the same fear over more trivial things.
Peter McWilliams and John Rogers

Remember, F.E.A.R. is a False Expectation About Risk

What you fear rarely ever happens. In his first few seasons, when ratings were low, Conan O'Brien feared his show was going to be canceled. Remember that Dorothy was scared of the great Oz until she pulled back the green curtain and discovered that her fears were unfounded. The fears you imagine are almost always just that—imagined.

Replace your fear with faith

The more you realize that your fears are mostly imaginary, the easier it gets to replace your fears with faith. "The whole secret of existence is to have no fear," Buddha said. Fear creates insecurity, lowers your confidence, and silences your heart. Worst of all it puts off bad vibes. It's been said that you attract what you fear. The more you can replace your fears with faith that things will work out, the more you'll live happy and powerful. Cheap Trick once sang, "Everything will work out if you let it. If you let it in your heart."

Here are five scenarios that may help you decide if you want to pursue the career that you really want.

1. Possible Failure—So What?

David Letterman's first television show was canceled due to bad ratings. At 22, Oprah Winfrey was fired from being an anchorwoman because of her inexperience. The first time Jay Leno performed his stand-up comedy routine for Johnny Carson, Johnny told him he wasn't good enough for a spot on the *Tonight Show*. Lucille Ball's first acting coach recommended that she find a different career, and she was fired from her first four chorus-line jobs.

"A person's ability to grow and succeed is directly related to their ability to suffer embarrassment," said Doug C. Engelbart, the father of personal computers. What Engelbart's quote implies is that mistakes and failure are necessary parts of achieving greatness. For myself, over and over I've had the experience of losing first and winning later. I was a bad long-distance runner before I was a good one. I gave embarrassing speeches before I gave highly praised ones. I made bad marketing materials before I made good ones. I wrote terrible cover letters before I wrote ones that

Do not fear failure—embrace it.
Conan O'Brien

The greatest mistake you can make in life is to be continually fearing you will make one.
Elbert Hubbard

Be braver—you can't cross a chasm in two small jumps.
Chinese proverb

Neither you nor the world knows what you can do until you have tried.
Ralph Waldo Emerson

won jobs. The moral of all those examples is this: Yes, you might have failures along the way. But those failures are precisely what give you the feedback you need to succeed.

Worst-case scenario: You don't achieve the level you wanted to attain. But even in this case you are guaranteed to grow more than others who didn't take risks, and you'll network with many people who can be helpful to your future. Not a bad return simply for trying.

2. It's Your Life—Go Live It

Daryl Hannah moved from Chicago to Hollywood against her parents' wishes and then became a movie star. Actor and director John Turturro's father didn't want him to go into acting. "Basically, he wanted me to be a doctor or a lawyer because I had good grades."

So somebody important to you thinks that your dream job is a really bad idea. Maybe it's your parents or a good friend. Take their reaction as a good sign. In the words of career consultant Howard Figler, "You want at least one person to disagree with your career choice so that you know you're doing your own thinking." People who care about you will often discourage you out of love, not logic. They want to protect you from fears that are real to them but not necessarily true threats to you. If you're in this situation, do this: Research the ins and outs thoroughly so you know the pluses and minuses better than those around you. If you decide it's worth the risks, tell the ones you love that you chose the career because you have more motivation for it than any other choice. Tell them that you researched the choice thoroughly and feel like it is worth the risks involved and assure them that you didn't make the choice to hurt their feelings. Then Go For It.

3. Never Mind Your Major

Jim Conlon went to Syracuse University and majored in history. Less than one year after graduating he had a job with an investment firm. Jennifer Scully was an English literature/European studies major at Vanderbilt University. Two years after graduating she's deputy director of trustee programs for the Democratic National Committee.

Uh-oh. You majored in business but now you wish you could be a fitness coach. Well, good news: Your major has very little to do with what jobs you can get. In a survey by the

Tips on How to Feel Less Embarrassed:
1. Assume the people laughing at you wouldn't even try what you're doing.
2. Know that most people admire you for trying.
3. Remember that learning requires mistakes.
4. Be glad you're not on national TV (unless you are).
5. Think that the whole idea of "embarrassing" is lame.
6. Believe that it's healthy to get a daily dose of embarrassment.

I'm blowing up my problems to the size of a cow.
Lyrics from "Size of a Cow"
by The Wonderstuff

Follow your own bent, no matter what people say.
Karl Marx, philosopher

College Review Board, knowledge of your major ranked eleventh on a list of what employers look for. In addition to that startling fact, consider the words of career expert Dave Swanson: "Seventy-five percent of jobs are filled by people without the proper degree or qualifications." My personal testimony to the truth of that statement is the fact that my first dream job was as a technology manager, despite the fact that I had majored in speech and communications. And I currently write and speak about professional development despite the fact that I had no college experience in the field of career development. Your major or your work experience doesn't have to limit you. People often pursue their dreams in spite of not having the proper experience.

4. A Shirt for Your Back

Robert Kiyosaki didn't buy into the myth that it's impossible to be a teacher and make lots of money. He was flat broke when he started teaching at age 32, and by 45 he was wealthy and financially independent. In his book *If You Want to Be Rich & Happy Don't Go to School* (Aslan, 1993), he says, "Even Peace Corps volunteers could be millionaires if they comprehended the principles [of money making]." The principles he's referencing will not be taught to you during college, but you can learn them for yourself in the short book *The Wealthy Barber* by David Chilton (Prima Publishing).

Does your dream job pay poorly? Don't let a low salary hold you back because there are many other ways to accumulate wealth. In addition to applying the principles for generating wealth that will make anyone on any income wealthy, remember to shop around because oftentimes the same job will pay significantly more in a different part of the country or world or in a different industry. Finally, remember that above the level of being able to afford food and shelter, happiness has very little to do with income.

5. You Can't Touch This

Finally, if you're being realistic, you have to acknowledge the factor of competition. But at the same time you also have to acknowledge a few other factors. First of all, consider the fact that we don't live in a world where you have to be the best, or even in the top 100, to be able to make a living at any certain profession. You wanna be a movie critic? You don't have to beat Roger Ebert to make a living at it.

As you attempt to make big differences, remember to appreciate the small differences. And remember that you don't always have to reach the goal you set in order to make a difference.
Win Borden

Money will come to you when you are doing the right thing.
Michael Phillips, writer

What's money? A man is a success if he gets up in the morning and goes to bed at night and in between does what he wants to do.
Bob Dylan, singer

Consider the enthusiasm factor. Maybe your dream job is very competitive, but you have more enthusiasm for that job than 95% of the other people applying. Enthusiasm is the greatest competitive advantage of all. Those working out of obligation run out of gas, while those operating on enthusiasm gain momentum.

Alan Kulwicki went into the astronomically competitive sport of stock car racing without any connections or money, in a sport that requires millions. He went about his goal with the attitude, "Maybe we can't win, but surely we'll lose if we don't try." Seven years after beginning his career he won the 1992 Winston Cup racing championship.

So with new insights into the fears we all face, you are in a better position to pursue your true passion. Before I move on to a discussion of how to pursue your passions, you'll benefit from knowing two simple things:

1. People who have reached great heights were not fearless. (In fact, it seems that the ones who make it are the ones who can move forward despite having fears.)

2. In the words of Theodore Roosevelt, "It's not the critic who counts or the person who pointed out how the strong person stumbled or where the doer of deeds could have done them better. The credit belongs to the person who is actually in the arena, whose face is marred by dust and sweat and blood; who strives valiantly; who errs and comes short again and again; who knows the great enthusiasms, the great devotions, and spends themself in a worthy cause; who at best knows the triumph of high achievement and who at the worst, if they fail, at least fails while daring greatly, so that their place will never be with those cold and timid souls, who know neither victory nor defeat."

In the next section of the book you're going to get your Action Plans. This is where things pick up speed. If your dream is to paint a masterpiece, you're going to start doing things that make you a great artist. If you're interested in helping people, you'll start taking actions that enable you to become great at helping people. If you're really interested in history and you dream of being wealthy, you're going to start doing things that will make you a high-paid historian.

When billionaire Henry Ford was asked what he would do if he lost all of his fortune, he replied, "I'd have it all back in five years."

I started to realize that people weren't as great as I had built them up to be. Just because someone was an attorney didn't make them any greater or smarter than me.

Karen Socher

You'll always have the edge if you think you're number one.

Harvey B. Mackay

Shut up and jump!

Bungee-jumping phrase

The most difficult thing is to just start the ball rolling. Once it starts, it's actually more difficult to stop it.

Butch Lovelace

But remember, the self-discovery process that you initiated in the previous chapters is a lifelong process that, when done with consistency, provides focus, motivation, and joy. Stay in the habit of journalizing. Reread the previous chapters occasionally. Keep getting clear on what you'd like out of life. You'll stay in touch with the number one success factor: extraordinary drive.

PART 2

Action Plan

Whatever you do or dream, you can begin it.
Boldness has genius, power and magic in it.
Begin it now.

Goethe, poet and dramatist

Rollin', Rollin', Rollin'!

With more clarity about your interests and dreams, you are out of the starting blocks and on the track. In the next section of this book, you're going to learn:

- how to go on great escapes and get academic credit for it
- the most enjoyable way to gain real skills during college
- how to put your grades in perspective
- the classes that will save your a—— later on in the working world
- how to do more—better, faster, and easier
- how to make college work for you
- where and how to get leadership training
- the fastest way to become good at anything
- how to do "reality checks" that might change your life
- how to strike "information gold" when it comes to being an expert
- how a childhood game can improve your success
- how you can "go pro" with one phone call

By the end of these chapters you'll know enough to get more out of college than 95% percent of the students around you. These chapters start with the story of a student who went to the other side of the world and then all the way to the White House.

CHAPTER 8

Great Escapes

Camille Cellucci was visual effects producer on the block-buster movie *Titanic*. Working side by side with director James Cameron was "an absolute dream come true." She had wanted to be a part of entertaining audiences since she was a little girl growing up in Reno, California.

> *I remember watching Red Skelton when I was three or four. I'd watch the audience respond to him and think to myself, "I want to do that." As a child I didn't have the words do describe it, but I wanted to be a part of creating an experience that allows people to take a break from everyday life. My mom kept thinking, "She'll want to be a ballerina or a fireman next week," but I never changed my mind.*

Working on *Titanic* made her a hot ticket in Hollywood, and it changed her life.

> *I learned so much from Jim [Cameron]. He's so passionate about his work. He was one of the first people to [have] faith in my creativity. That faith gave me the confidence to take risks on my own, writing and directing. So Titanic changed my life by moving me to work on my own dreams, visions, and projects.*

Camille went to UC Berkeley and was a film and social science major. How did she get to work on such a blockbuster film? For starters, while she was in college she created her own internship at Industrial Light and Magic (ILM), the special effects house that made *Star Wars*.

> *During my senior year I applied at ILM without telling them I was still in school. When I mentioned that I would*

I *don't* believe there's such a thing as the biggest mistake of your life, because you can always learn something.

Camille Cellucci

45

need Tuesdays and Thursdays off they found out I was a student. My chances of getting hired were over. So I suggested that I create an internship program for them. I had already done an internship with an ABC television station so I was able to ask my friends there for help with the legalities of an internship program.

Camille was determined to make it happen. She kept saying to herself, "It's bulldog time. Somehow, I'm going to make this happen. I don't know how, but I will." She called and told the person at ILM that she'd intern for free. She got the internship. She even got paid. It was an exciting day, to say the least.

Near the end of her year-long internship she was supposed to get her big break—working as a production assistant on the movie *Star Trek IV.* But at the last minute, ILM didn't get the *Star Trek* job. However, fate had it that a receptionist who had just been hired didn't show up, and Camille was quick to volunteer for the position.

> When I was leaving for France and saying goodbye I thought, "I must be crazy." I had lots of fears. It was huge to leave my friends for a year. And definitely there were times that were hard—like being homesick. But it was so worth it.
>
> *Camille Cellucci*

I wasn't above anything. I covered the phones, I got coffee, I shredded paper. Then, after six months, I was supposed to get my big break as a production assistant on the film Ghostbusters II, *where I would supposedly move up to a coordinator role quickly. But again at the last minute, I was put on a movie called* The Abyss. *I didn't want to work on* The Abyss. *I really wanted to work on* Ghostbusters II *and I was a wreck over it. I could never have imagined at the time that* The Abyss *would lead me to working on* Titanic. *Had I not worked on* The Abyss, *which was a James Cameron film, I would not have been the visual effects producer on* Titanic. *From this, I learned that things can seem really unfair and not make sense while they're happening to you, but you just don't have all the information yet. It could lead to the biggest thing that's ever happened to you in your life.*

> There's a level at which I became street smart from living overseas.
>
> *Camille Cellucci*

Surprisingly, when Camille announced her intention to leave a great job for her role on *Titanic* she was bombarded with warnings.

When I went to work on Titanic, *everybody thought it was going to be a giant flop. Studio executives sat me down to show me why it was going to be a horrible failure and the biggest mistake of my life—and these were people that sincerely cared about me. But my gut and my heart kept saying, "It's a risk you've got to take. There is something about this film and working with Jim that you have to do." That's what my heart would say when I got really quiet. So I did it.*

In an odd twist of fate, *Titanic* used ILM to produce many of their special effects, so Camille found herself in the position of hiring the people who had employed her as an intern. She had come full circle.

So what experience during school is Camille most grateful for? Surprisingly, it is the year she lived and studied abroad in France.

A year overseas was definitely helpful in job interviews because people were interested in it.
Camille Cellucci

I recommend everyone go study abroad. It was an invaluable experience. Not only was it one of the best years of my life, but it also gave me a new sense of independence and self-assurance. Bar none, bonding with my host family was the highlight of the trip—to realize you can create family anywhere. It gave me a sense of being able to feel safe anywhere in the world. It's so comforting to know you'll find your way and be all right. You'll find people you care about and who care about you.

Camille didn't just stay in France.

A friend of mine from Reno happened to be living in another city in France. We took a month and did the Euro-rail thing. We went to Switzerland, Greece, Italy, Spain—all over Europe. It was fantastic! After having traveled all over with a backpack and very little money, coming back and taking on challenges I'd never faced before was much easier. I had much more confidence.

Were there some moments that Camille will never forget?

Just learning to speak another language has brought so many incredible experiences into my life that otherwise wouldn't have happened.
Camille Cellucci

Before going overseas I'd heard the French don't shower everyday because water is a lot more expensive. I'd heard they'd buy fine clothing and wear it four days in a row. When I first got there, I was trying to be really good by showering only once a week. Three months into it I got sick and had to stay home for a few days. I was surprised to hear the shower running four days in a row. Very gently, not wanting to offend her, I asked my French-mom, "I'm just curious, are you guys showering everyday?" She replied, "Of course." I explained and she said, "We just thought showering once a week was your way!" We both howled with laughter.

Does Camille have any thoughts on pursuing a very cool job?

Yes. Trust your instincts and follow your heart. I don't know about other lifetimes or where we're headed, but we're here on the planet now and we're incredibly lucky. If you really want to do something you should do it—use all your power to do it. I never even thought of doing special effects. I just knew I wanted to do film and I stuck to that. It led me on this amazing journey.

Studying overseas for a semester is an invaluable experience. There are two ways to look at going overseas. From your perspective and from an employer's perspective. Let's start with your perspective.

Plain and simple there is no better reason to go overseas than the sheer fun of it. Every student I've ever met who did a semester abroad remembers it as the single best experience they had in college. They describe the exciting travels they did to global hot spots like Camden Market in London or the Indian Beer House in Taiwan or the Hamburg Fish Market in Germany or the Bastille in Paris or the Harajuku in Tokyo. Then in the next breath they mention the friends they made and the interesting people they met.

After hearing them talk about their experience, you begin to wonder if they went to classes at all! But yes they did, and then they always have stories to tell about studying and school. For those who might be intimidated by studying in a foreign country, take note of what student Jennifer Scully said about her overseas experience in France.

I had six years of French, but when I got there it didn't mean anything. When I got there I felt like a babe in the woods. The first several weeks I had no idea what they were saying. I really didn't. I would try to take notes and it was gibberish and I thought, "I'm going to flunk out. I can't do this. I've got to go home." And then it was almost like driving a stick shift—suddenly I was just doing it! Suddenly I was just understanding what they were saying. These

---

Two things got me really excited about the progress I was making on speaking French: I got a joke and I dreamed in French!

Camille Cellucci

You really can't understand the United States until you've been able to look at it from the perspective of other traditions, customs, and values. This is perhaps where I gained the most from my experience abroad.

Trevver Buss, University of Wisconsin–Madison graduate

words were coming out my mouth. I started dreaming in French. You know it just happened. That's immersion. That's the only way to do it!

Amazingly student testimonials don't end with travels, friends, and studies. Many students rave about the work experience they got overseas; some do office work in a city's downtown, while others do environmental work in a field in the country. Take, for example, California State University–Chico graduate Tim De Voe, who helped restore a habitat for waterfowl in the hay fields of Holland.

Our work provided continual opportunities to get to know one another and to share our cultures. Much of this took place in the flat-bottomed, open-air boat that helped us navigate the canal networks. Weekends gave us a chance to leave rural Holland behind and experience other aspects of Dutch culture. Highlights included a visit to a beach near The Hague (where swimming and sunning attire is definitely different than it is in the U.S.!) and to the National Park De Hoge Veluwe near Apeldoorn, where we gaped at artwork by Picasso, Braque, Redon, and Van Gogh. Reflecting back on it, my experience at the work camp was one of the best I have ever had.

Add it all up and in the end why do most of them feel it was the best experience they had in college? One student, Trevver Buss, who studied abroad in Australia, summed it up pretty well by saying, "You'll learn the usual classroom stuff, but the education you get from the people and culture of another country can never be copied in a $50, ten-pound textbook with shiny covers."

On the other hand, how do employers look at overseas experience? Employers love to find students who have studied abroad and here's why. First off, it tells them that they've found a person with a broad perspective. Having a perspective that is larger than a college campus or even a city is important to employers because companies now do business in a global economy. Employees who have global experience are just what companies of today need. It says to an employer that you have had experience adapting to new and unfamiliar circumstances. The ability to adapt to new situations is very appealing to employers because it tells them that no matter what changes come up in your job—people changes

Walking to work is a real education, with all the posters and different designs you see. It's great to get another perspective on the things I've learned in school.
Maria Lauengco, Ohio University graduate who worked abroad as a computer graphic artist

Having a keen interest in English literature, exploring places like Stratford (the birthplace of Shakespeare) and Brontë country really appealed to me.
Pam Livingstone, University of Illinois graduate and English major

It isn't what you know that counts; it's what you think of in time.
Unknown

You'll have a new way of looking at the world—and yourself—once you've adapted to a new environment and culture. You will open up a whole new world for yourself.
Trevver Buss

or responsibility changes—you will be able to adapt without too much trouble. That's a big deal to employers because many employees can't adapt. Last but not least, overseas experience tells an employer that you can deal with problems. One thing is for sure, not everything goes smoothly when you're studying or traveling in a country that is foreign to you. When employers see that you've been overseas, they know that you've learned a lot about dealing with challenges.

Benefits you get from studying or working abroad for a semester

- fun! fun! fun!
- cool! cool! cool!
- new friends
- encounters with interesting people
- increased self-confidence
- larger historical perspective
- strengthening of a foreign language (if English isn't the primary language)
- weekend travel to other interesting places
- problem-solving skills
- time away from where you are now
- a global perspective
- dramatic improvement of your mind, abilities, and life!
- great experience to add to your resume

How to study or work abroad

You can choose to study abroad for a semester or during summer or winter breaks. Here's how to get started:

Start by finding out if your school has a foreign exchange program (look in your course catalog or call an academic advisor). For instance, Rockford College in Illinois makes it easy for students to study for a semester at Regent's College in London, for no additional tuition or fees. This is often called a sister school relationship. In most cases, you'll receive academic credit from a sponsoring college or university and you'll be assisted and supervised by a resident staff.

If your school doesn't have an exchange program, call CIEE (Council on International Educational Exchange) at

Some people never go crazy. What horrible lives they must lead.

Charles Bukowski

If you listen to my first record, you'll wonder, "How did this guy last in the music business for 20 years?" I'm very tenacious. It goes back to that line in *Cool Hand Luke,* "You're gonna have to kill me to get me to quit."

John Mellencamp

Remember, you can't steer a parked car.

Anonymous

(212) 822-2600. Ask for their free guide *Basic Facts on Study Abroad*. Also make sure to get the latest issue of CIEE's magazine *Student Travels*, as well as their *Work Abroad* brochure and a catalog of their many books. CIEE administers 41 study abroad programs in 21 countries that are sponsored cooperatively by colleges and universities.

More than 5,000 students (and recent graduates) work overseas through the CIEE's Work Abroad program per year. Application procedures are simple—just fill out a one-page form. No minimum G.P.A. is needed, and for most of the programs, there is no language requirement. Typical job positions American students find are as secretaries, chambermaids, office workers, hotel clerks, and fruit pickers, but the pay is usually enough to cover your living expenses and enable you to go on a fair number of weekend excursions.

How Much It Costs

Whether you're studying abroad or working abroad, it's easy to cover your living expenses. Remember, studying and working are different than traveling abroad. Traveling is much more expensive. That's why it's best to see different countries through work or study programs. Costs may vary depending on what school you're attending and what country you choose to study in, but for the most part it's inexpensive (it becomes more expensive after you graduate). If you're there on a work program you'll usually make the same amount of money you'd make working here in the States. Would you rather work in the same joint you worked in last summer or get off work and walk home through the streets of London?

My Own Regrets

I didn't study abroad and I feel like I missed out. I can't believe I didn't go—especially considering that my college had many different study abroad programs that I could have taken advantage of at very little additional cost. Now that I've heard so many of my peers speak so highly about their experiences, I really regret not having gone to study in London or Mexico. My friend David Thompson went to study for a semester in Germany, and I can testify by his postcards and stories that he had a much better semester than all of us back home.

Next you'll find out how a 24-year-old college graduate had the know-how to launch a big-time national magazine.

▶ **HOT TIP**

Call for CIEE's FREE guide: *Basic Facts on Study Abroad*, 1-888-COUNCIL (Toll free in the U.S.) or (212) 822-2600. Or check out CIEE on the Web, ciee.org.

▶ **HOT TIP**

CIEE's FREE guide to educational programs in the Third World contains a listing of programs in Africa, Asia, and Latin America. And there are grants available for those thinking about studying in one of these countries. Ask for CIEE's FREE *Travel Grants for Educational Programs in the Third World*.

▶ **HOT TIP**

If you don't have time for a semester, you can choose a 3 to 8 week language and culture program in China, France, Japan, Russia, Spain, or the United Kingdom through CIEE.

▶ **HOT TIP**

www.studyabroad.com is a terrific new source for a vast amount of information about studying abroad. Maybe all the info you'll need!

CHAPTER 9

Work Hard, Play Hard

At only 24, David Eggers was the editor of *Might*, a new magazine available nationally. The first issue began with:

Yeah, yea. **Another** *twentysomething magazine—who needs it? What is* **Might** *and what does it want? And who wants* **Might**? *Who would read a magazine with a streaker on the cover? And where are the celebrities? The bands? The sex?* **Might** *is for young people, but there's no beauty tips, no dating hints or articles about partying. What gives? Where's the fashion? Where's the consumer guide? The fads? The models? The hype? The unreadable type? Could there really be more to a generation than illiterate, uninspired, flannel-wearing "slackers"? Could a generation really consist of 47 million* **different** *people? Could a bunch of people under 25 put out a national magazine with no corporate backing and no clue about marketing? With a shoe string budget and an unpaid staff? With actual views and actual issues? With a sense of purpose and a sense of humor? With guts and goals and hope? Who would* **read** *a magazine like that? You might.*

David Eggers wrote that introduction and started *Might* with two friends. On the side, he has his own comic strip running in a San Francisco newspaper and he's working on his painting abilities.

> Often the writing I do sucks and it gets rejected. Just last week I did two illustrations where someone important told me, "These are bad. Really, really bad." It did hurt. You need pretty thick skin.
>
> *David Eggers, editor of* Might *magazine*

I make lists of things I want to do. For instance, years ago I put on my list that it would be great to have a syndicated cartoon or a published magazine. I'm trying to live as rich and as varied a life as I can.

David graduated from the University of Illinois with a degree in journalism.

The University of Illinois wasn't my first choice. I imagined myself at an Ivy League school, but after I got rejected by Brown University and wait-listed by Cornell, I found myself in the cornfields of Illinois. It took me a long time to get used to it.

Diversify—don't put all your eggs in one basket. *SF Weekly* could call and say "We hate your cartoon" and it wouldn't kill me because I have ten other things going on.
David Eggers

Being involved in extracurricular activities helped David settle in. Over the course of his college career, he got involved in several things: working on the campus newspaper, running the campus art gallery, participating in the campus concert promotions, taking art and design classes at Chicago Art Institute, and completing a summer internship at *Chicago* magazine.

We work 60 to 70 hours a week but it's fine, because for us this is work, leisure, and fun all rolled into one.
David Eggers

I wanted my extracurricular activities and my summer jobs to advance my career. I saw a lot of students pick interesting majors but not think at all about what they needed to do in order to make their major practical. I was inspired by a visiting professor who, in addition to being a teacher, had an exciting career as a journalist and an artist. A fax would come in for him from the New York Times *with a design job. He'd cancel class, do the design, fax it back, and the next day you'd see it in the* New York Times. *On top of this, his art was being shown in different galleries around the world! Watching him I learned that you have to work your ass off. And most importantly, I saw how much you can do, how many people you can touch, and how fulfilling it can be.*

Bite off more than you can chew, then chew like hell.
Peter Brock

So how did he get *Might* magazine started?

After working at a few different jobs after college, a high school friend and I just decided to do it. It was an idea we'd had for a while, and we were prodded or inspired by every magazine we'd see.

What made him think he could pull it off?

I picked up a lot of skills through my extracurricular activities in college, like computers, production, photography, and journalism, so I had some basis for my confidence. Of *course, there have been a lot of obstacles, like raising the $10,000 we needed to do the first issue, but in the end it's "How bad do you want it?"*

Clubs and volunteer work are where the action is. They can provide opportunities to:

- meet and make great friends

- learn a lot more about your interests

- start accomplishing your dreams

- gain the experience that employers and graduate schools look for

- do cool things like see guest speakers, put on events, work with money

- make a difference

- network with accomplished professionals

- take all-expense-paid trips to interesting conferences

- network to jobs in the real world

David Eggers isn't the only recent graduate who leveraged his campus club experience into success. As you read about the other notable people whose stories are in this book, you'll find that all of them except one participated in campus clubs. And the one exception was Michael Bates, a student who was in and out of college in a total of two and a half years. So it's safe to say that campus club experiences have helped a lot of very successful people get to where they are.

For instance, shortly after graduating college Simon Tonner became marketing director for the computer book publisher Ziff-Davis Press. During his college days at San Francisco State University, he was the president of the Advertising Club. As an officer of the club he did many things, from making flyers to organizing fundraising events. But best of all, he and five other students from the club entered a contest to create an ad campaign for a line of Chevrolet cars. Together they made up a possible campaign, from the slogans to the commercials, and pitched it to a group of advertising executives from San Francisco. It's no wonder Simon got a great job in marketing after college—by the time he graduated he'd already gotten some real experience.

Dennis is such a participator. He's willing to be bad at anything for a while, and then he gets great at it. So therefore he can do almost anything!

Meg Ryan, describing her husband, Dennis Quaid

I try not to leave things to chance. For instance, I like writing articles but instead of hoping that a magazine will publish them, I started my own.

David Eggers

▶ **HOT TIP**

Don't subject yourself to anyone who doesn't believe in, or encourage you to go all the way with, your ambitions.

If advertising doesn't turn your crank, imagine having this experience next semester: You attend a three-day conference in a different city where hundreds of other students are also in attendance. There you take skill-building workshops; watch comedians, musicians, jugglers, sword duelers, hypnotists, psychics, motivational speakers, and fire eaters perform; and then schedule your favorite performers for a show at your school. In many colleges, students who are involved in the Student Activities Club do this—and more—every year.

Sometimes campus clubs give you more than just great experience—sometimes they give you connections. Michael Minjares, coordinator for Student Enrichment at San Diego State, sees this happen all the time. He told me about Stephanie, a student who worked in the summer as an orientation leader assisting new students and their parents. One day while working the Parent Program, Stephanie was talking about life as a business major and her future career plans. It just so happened that in the parent audience was a gentleman who was involved in the same organization Stephanie desired to join. Impressed with Stephanie's communication and leadership skills, the parent approached Stephanie immediately after the presentation to offer her a business card and a chance to interview with his company. Booya! Why didn't someone tell me how GREAT it is to get involved in campus clubs?!!!!!

Find out what clubs and volunteer programs there are on your campus. Ask at the counseling center or look in the course catalog. You're likely to find that there are many organizations that would match your interests. For instance:

Accounting	Marketing
Advertising	Nursing homes
Agriculture	Photography
AIDS programs	Planned Parenthood
Alcohol awareness	Radio
Art	Red Cross
Children's centers	Social work
Clubs that serve a specific ethnicity	Student activities
Community health	Student government
Economics	Student orientation
Environmental clubs	Teaching
Homeless shelters	Theater
Hospital care	Women's issues
Journalism	Writing

In today's economy there are no experts, no "best and brightest" with all the answers. It's up to each one of us. The only way to screw up is to not try anything.
Tom Peters

I think TV is great. When I'm in a hotel room, I sit there and try all these new channels and see what's going on. I probably stay up too late watching stuff. TV is neat. I don't have a TV at home, because I prefer to spend that time thinking—or mostly reading. So I'm pretty conscious about not letting myself get used to certain things.
Bill Gates, CEO and Chairman of the Board of Microsoft Corp.

Opportunity is missed by most people because it is dressed in overalls and looks like work.
Thomas Edison, inventor

This is just a sample list. In case your school doesn't have the club you'd like to be in, remember you can start your own. Schools always have procedures for helping students start up a new club.

Great lines for your resume!

Students consistently report that being involved in student organizations was one of the most enjoyable things they did in college. But enjoying college more isn't the only benefit; there are also benefits for your future employment. As you learned in the first section of this book, employers are looking for a lot more than good grades and a degree these days. Extracurricular involvement is one thing that employers love to see and your resume will shine with lines like these after you've been involved in campus clubs:

- "Managed revenues and funds. Developed and implemented programs to promote diversity education" (for those who were involved in a campus club that educated the student body).

- "Counseled, aided, and advised new students" (for those who got involved in freshman orientation).

- "Planned and coordinated weekly meetings involving up to 40 students and a guest speaker from the business community" (for those who planned meetings that included guest speakers).

- "Coordinated annual banquet" (for those who planned the end-of-the-year party).

- "Created and developed organizational selection recruitment and publicity" (for those who made posters and flyers and placed ads in the campus newspaper to get students to join club/organization).

- "Developed and implemented organizational selection procedures" (for those who planned the selection of new members).

- "Coordinated major public events, including national acts such as comedian Rob Schneider and rock band the Kinks. Comanaged $50,000 budget" (for those who were involved in student activities).

Don't tell me I'm burning the candle at both ends—tell me where to get more wax!!

Unknown

Life is like a game of cards. The hand that is dealt you represents determinism; the way you play it is free will.

Jawaharial Nehru

In a nutshell, after you've joined a campus club, your experience will say to an employer:

- This person is well rounded.

- This person has some real experience that will help him or her on the job.

- This person is self-motivated.

- This person can work in teams.

- This person may or may not have a pet. (Just checking your reflexes.)

Make it work for your dreams

Use campus club involvement to accomplish your dreams. If your dream is to improve race relations in the world, then get involved in, or start, a campus club that focuses on improving race relations on your campus. This is how you'll find other people that share your dream. This is where you get resources like money, people, information, and connections. If what you think should be changed in the world is better treatment of the elderly, then volunteer at a nursing home. The day you start volunteering is the day the treatment of elderly people gets a little bit better. It's also the day you move one step closer to accomplishing your dream on a large scale.

In case you were wondering how it would be humanly possible to be active in campus clubs while also maintaining that Dean's List G.P.A., next you'll read about a college student who didn't think getting straight A's was very important and who went on to be CEO of a $12 million company.

To refuse the adventure is to run the risk of drying up like a pea in a shell.

George Mallory, mountaineer

Killing time is not murder, it is suicide.

John Mason

CHAPTER 10

Never Mind the Grades

Michael Bates is rich at 29, but money isn't what motivates him.

I'll work around the clock on problems that are challenging, things that other people think can't be done, because for me, that's the ultimate fun. As for money, it comes when you're endeavoring to do your best at what you enjoy. And of course it's fun to make a lot of money, but it's not just money that makes me happy. The best part of my life is getting to work with a team of people that I admire and respect, who are focused on the same goals.

What you major in during college has no bearing on what careers you can do afterwards.

Michael Bates

Michael went to college at Arizona State University and graduated with a mediocre grade point average of about 2.5.

I have a short attention span. I get bored very easily, and I can't spell worth a darn. But I'd find ways around my weaknesses to get papers done. I'd get a buddy of mine who was a good speller to type our papers while I'd dictate them.

I've bombed in several businesses. The first software company I was in I made the mistake of signing personal guarantees for advertising and promotion. When the company went belly up they came after me for hundreds of thousands of dollars.

Michael Bates

Actually, Michael's G.P.A. wasn't an overriding concern because his focus was elsewhere: Starting up his own business of buying and selling used cars for a profit.

If I saw an opportunity, I took it. I was importing green market Mercedes and Porsches from Europe and buying and selling used cars. Used cars were 40% cheaper in Europe, and all I had to do was modify a few things and then I could sell them for a profit.

What business classes did he take during college?

I didn't take a single business course in college. I learned what I know from trial and failure. I fail all the time. The first thing I really botched up was my attempt to buy and sell cars. The first car I bought was a lemon, a bad car. From there I had to learn the mechanics of cars in order to be successful at that business. Getting back to the fact that I didn't take a single business course: I have seen a lot of business professors go through college, do their bachelor's, their master's, and then their Ph.D. and only come out with a lot of textbook business knowledge. But ask them how to build a business from zero cash flow and they wouldn't know how to do it.

After a few years of entrepreneurial ups and downs, Michael figured out how to build a business from basically nothing. He started Software Marketing Corp., the company he is now CEO of, at age 26, in an upstairs room of his house, with only $200. By the time Michael was 29 Software Marketing Corp. was a $12 million company.

Any advice for college students?

I've had at least a five-year plan since the time I was 16. I'd think about where I wanted to be a year from now, three years from now, and five years from now. I liked thinking about the big picture rather than the next exam because it made immediate tasks and pressures look like stepping stones towards my future.

How are you doing in school?

We usually answer that question immediately with thoughts about our grades. Grades, grades, grades! Their importance has been deeply ingrained in most of us. It seems like completing your assignments and getting good grades is the urgent bottom line in college. It's easy to feel like good grades are your golden ticket to success. But, there is more than one side to this story. Many people don't need good grades in order to be successful.

Before I lay out the reason why you might not need good grades in order to succeed, let me state the reasons why you might in fact need high marks. First of all, you may have

I make a very dumb decision at least once a week.

Michael Bates

I drive at night—that's my thinking time.

Michael Bates

▶ **HOT TIP**

Great books for entrepreneurs, self-employed and independent contractors:

• *Entrepreneurs Are Made, Not Born* by Lloyd Shetsky

• *Running a One Person Business* by Claude Whitmyer, Salli Rasberry, and Michael Phillips

• *Making It on Your Own: Surviving and Thriving on the Ups and Downs of Being Your Own Boss* by Paul and Sarah Edwards

• *National Business Employment Weekly Guide to Self-Employment* by David Lord

There are two thoughts that will ensure success in all you do: (1) Don't tell everything you know, and (2) until *Ace Ventura,* no actor had considered talking through his ass.

Jim Carrey

▶ **HOT TIP**

Things that make them go hmmm ... key words like
• president
• manager
• editor
• chairperson
• captain
• Phi Beta Kappa
These get recruiters to sit up and take notice.

Source: Campus Connections *magazine, published by MarketSource Corp.*

▶ **HOT TIP**

Your Guide to Getting Better Grades Using the Internet and Online Services—A Michael Wolff Book

grade requirements imposed on you by outside forces such as financial aid institutions, scholarship funding, club membership, or parental orders. Secondly, you may desire to attend a graduate school that requires a certain G.P.A. Thirdly, you may just care so much about getting great grades that you can't imagine being able to hold your head up in public without them. If one of these descriptions is you, then you'll probably be best served by continuing to make sure that your grades are high.

But what if you didn't fall into one of the above situations? What if you're striving for great grades simply because you want to do a good job in school? If this is you, STOP and reconsider, because straight A's will put you at the top of the heap during college, but after college the rules of the game shift dramatically. And if you focus all of your attention on excelling at homework and tests, after graduation you might feel like you're suited up for football but are stuck in a basketball game. Let me explain.

The vast majority of employers will not ask you about your grades *unless* they have nothing else to evaluate you by, which is why work experience, internships, and co-op education are so very important. Hard to believe that most employers don't care about your grades? In a recent study by the College Review Board that asked businesses what they want, employers mentioned ten other things before they mentioned G.P.A. Yes, good grades can help indicate to someone that you are disciplined, but if you believe that grades are important outside of academia, you misunderstand how things really work. In academic professions such as teaching, science, or research-oriented work, grades are considered important, but if you're planning to work outside of the college/university environment, you may want to consider what many people have learned: SINCE GRADUATING, NOBODY HAS ASKED ME ABOUT MY G.P.A.

HEY! This chapter isn't trying to give you an excuse to get bad grades, this chapter is trying to give you logical reasons to allocate your valuable time and energy toward extracurricular activities such as campus clubs, internships, volunteer efforts, or entrepreneurial ventures. From experience, I know that many people don't choose to get involved in these things precisely because they take time and energy away from getting good grades. But hear this: It's a mistake to bet all your money on good grades. Grades aren't everything.

In the words of Scott Edelstein, author of *The Truth About College,* "For every successful person who had a high grade point average in college, there's another happy or successful person whose grades were mediocre or unexceptional."

You can always be successful without good grades. But you can't be successful without high self-esteem. Sometimes good grades require such an enormous struggle that your self-esteem and happiness suffer. Don't let this happen. Instead, shift your focus more towards extracurricular activities. You're likely to feel better about yourself and find areas where you really excel. Consider the testimony of a U.C. Berkeley student who had just won the award for the graduating senior with the highest G.P.A. "In looking back, I'm sad I won it. I could have gotten a 3.5 and still had time to live a normal life. While most other students developed social and leadership skills by joining clubs or other activities, I was busy making sure I didn't get a B on a test."

Don't have regrets when you graduate. The Berkeley student is right in saying that a great G.P.A. is not worth sacrificing enjoyable, important things like social and leadership activities. Especially since the achievement of good grades is often the result of completely absurd circumstances. For instance:

- Susan took U.S. history, thought it was a boring subject, and didn't learn anything she'll remember or use. But Susan was great at memorizing things—like the 50 states and key historical dates—so she got an A in the class.

- In one class, everyone knew that in order to get a good grade, you mostly needed to turn in a paper that was at least 20 pages in length with very few grammatical errors. It didn't really matter what you wrote in it.

- John took algebra and learned more than he'd ever learned before from a class. Unfortunately, because of his obligations to an internship, John did not have time to do all his homework assignments so he got a C.

- A professor did a poor job teaching the subject matter and gave a test that nobody was ready for. Paul didn't study an ounce, cheated on the test, and got an A. Karen studied all week, didn't cheat on the test, and got a D.

I always thought the only purpose of going to class was to get an A. I understand now that it's good to get an A, but it's also good to actually get something out of the class.

Derek Caracciolo,
communication arts major

Find something you are good at, work at it, and eventually you can succeed and make your life. Don't just slack off and think that you will just go through life doing a job. Try to do incredible things—put a lot of hours into making a lot of things very, very good.

Steve Wozniak,
creator of the Apple computer

- Dana took Spanish and learned to speak it well, better than many of the other students. But Dana got an F because he missed more than five days of class because of his involvement in a campus club.

- Amy wrote a tremendous paper that demonstrated incredible comprehension of and her great ideas about the subject matter. But she had too many grammatical errors so she got a C.

- Jamal learned a lot in his communications course but he clashed with the professor, who didn't seem to like students who had their own opinions. This personality clash resulted in Jamal getting a C instead of a B.

If I could do it over, I would get involved in student activities. That's the best education.

Karen Socher

I wish there was a knob on the TV to turn up the intelligence. There's a knob called "brightness," but it doesn't work.

Gallagher

Grades, grades, grades. How can you keep them in proper perspective? Start by remembering Michael Bates's suggestion to focus on the bigger picture and answer the infamous question "How are you doing in school?" with something like "I'm doing great in school. I'm in a campus club. I'm doing an excellent internship. I'm majoring in a subject that really interests me. I'm developing skills that are going to make me really valuable to employers. And most of my professors admire me, even if I'm not getting straight A's because they recognize that I'm learning the most."

Decide as soon as possible if you're going to work in the fields that require a postgraduate degree, like education or scientific research. If you are going to go into one of these fields, keep your grades as high as you need to. Often graduate schools require the combination of good grades and extracurricular activities.

If you plan to enter the working world after college, don't sweat your grades so much that they restrict your involvement in extracurriculars. A 3.0 is good. It will keep you in good academic standing and, when coupled with strong extra-curricular activities on your resume, will rank as acceptable at many graduate schools if you later choose that route.

If participating in extracurricular activities is having a negative impact on your grades, don't panic. Recognize that racking up time in an extracurricular activity such as an internship, campus club, or a real-world job is usually well worth the difference between getting a B instead of an A. Getting anything below a C is simply shooting yourself in the foot because it gets you on academic probation and even employers will interpret it as a sign that you can't handle all the responsibilities you take on.

Also, if you're worried about running into an employer who does ask about your grades, remember that this isn't likely to happen if you've got a resume full of extracurriculars and internships. However, if it does happen you can explain less-than-perfect grades by saying something like: "My G.P.A. was a 3.0 and I'll tell you why it wasn't higher. In addition to learning in the classroom, I also felt it was important to invest time and energy into extracurricular activities so that my classroom knowledge would be balanced with real-world abili-ties and skills. So in addition to my studies, I got involved in a campus club and an internship." A smart employer will be impressed.

Finally, remember while you're in college that getting good grades feels like the winning strategy. But in reality, you could complete every assignment, receive straight A's, and still be no closer to a happy life than before you began col-lege. If you don't drive yourself crazy trying for the coveted 4.0, you free up time that can be better used.

The next time you feel the urge to procrastinate...just put it off.
Unknown

Elvis Got an F in Music

And Nine Other Truths About Grades

- Good grades won't guarantee you happiness, success, or a good job after graduation.

- Grades have very little impact on most students' lives after they leave college.

- If you're going on to graduate school, or to work in academia, your G.P.A. is important.

- If you don't get passing grades, you can't proceed to the next level.

- Grades don't measure intuition, creativity, people skills, or entrepreneurial potential.

- "I got straight A's" is not a good pick-up line.

- Grading isn't solely based on what you learn—often it's based on other things (attendance, personality, paper length, memorization, discrimination, obedience).

- How much you're learning is a better indicator of your future success than your grades.

- Some professors will give you a C when you have learned a lot. Other professors will give you an A when you have learned very little.

- Elvis got an F in music.

Next up: A course-by-course description of the classes that will open doors for you right after college. This is one course catalog you don't want to miss.

CHAPTER 11

Classes Worth Their Weight in Gold

Not all classes are created equal. Some classes in particular will help you excel in your career. Here are the college courses that are highly likely to come in handy immediately following your graduation:

Business-Writing Course

While college may teach you to write academically, usually exploring a subject in-depth using an advanced vocabulary, businesses and organizations need you to be able to write papers that are short, simple, and to the point. As a matter of fact, the ability to communicate effectively has been consistently ranked as the number one performance factor for professional success. If you want to look good to your future employers, take a business-writing course. The course usually covers how to write memos, reports, and business letters.

Grant-Writing Course

Being able to get free money to help you do the work of your dreams is a reality if you know how to apply for grants. What is a grant? Let's say you become very rich running a magazine and decide that you want to give $5,000 a year to help other people start magazines. That $5,000 is called a grant and is given to the person with the best application. Now, here's the great part—there are grants for almost everything! In 1998 alone, grants from U.S. foundations totaled $20 billion and the grants were given to assist every purpose under the sun! Once you've completed a grant-writing course, you'll know how to find and apply for the grant money. Knowing how to apply for grant money is a valuable skill that many businesses need and pay money for. When I was at Levi Strauss & Co.,

▶ **HOT TIP**

Overenroll at class registration and then drop the classes with bad professors.

Academic prose often violates ordinary standards of "good" writing, such as plain language and a conversational tone. At best this style can be described as formal; at worst it is jargon-filled, abstract, stilted, and pompous.
Adam Robinson, author of
What Smart Students Know
(Crown)

▶ **HOT TIP**

Save the papers that you do in a business-writing course for interview show-and-tell items.

▶ **HOT TIP**

Look up grant information by asking at your library for directories on foundation funding, or by writing or calling the Foundation Center Library, 312 Sutter Street, Suite 312, San Francisco, CA 94108, (415) 397-0903 and requesting their catalog of books. fdncenter.org

Success isn't magic, but then magic isn't magic either.

somebody just out of college got hired specifically because of their grant-writing skills. Levi Strauss, like many large companies, has a department that gives away grant money. In addition, it might be your key to having the money you need to do the work of your dreams.

Promotions/Public Relations Course

Take a course that covers paid and unpaid activities designed to encourage the purchase of products and services including advertising, display, publicity/press releases, public relations, packaging, special events, and sale promotions. I encourage you to take a public relations course because you'll find that all companies can benefit from good public relations. Taking this course could open up a lot of job opportunities for you.

Speech/Business Presentations Course

Take a course that includes discussions and practice on delivering persuasive speeches, body language, assertive communications, and audiovisual aids. I've said it before and it's important enough to repeat: THE ABILITY TO COMMUNICATE EFFECTIVELY HAS BEEN CONSISTENTLY RANKED THE NUMBER ONE PERFORMANCE FACTOR FOR PROFESSIONAL SUCCESS. In our society, shyness is not considered an asset. A speech course can help you feel confident speaking to one or 1,000. And you can apply this confidence to situations that occur more often than in public speaking: speaking well over the phone; speaking up in class; making a good impression in an interview; and expressing your ideas in a meeting.

Sales/Selling Principles Course

Sales courses are helpful to everyone no matter what their professional aspirations. A good sales course will cover customer service, the processes and techniques of selling, time and activity planning, product/service knowledge, supporting activities, and managing the selling function. In addition to being a valuable skill in every field, knowing how to sell yourself is the key to winning the jobs and salaries that you desire. Studies suggest that you're going to need to win at least ten different jobs during your lifetime. So remember, if you can't sell yourself or your ideas, nobody will buy your services.

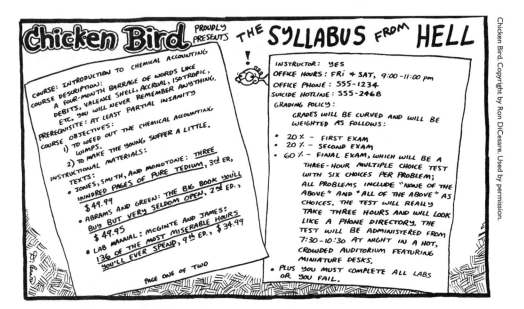

Time Management Workshop

Time management is a great tool everyone can use to work more effectively. You need to develop a system that allows you to get the most done in the least time. It's a wonder that it's not a required course for college students because it's practically a required skill in the real world.

Human Relations/Interpersonal Communications Course

Master the ability to get along well with almost anybody in everyday business and social situations. Develop the ability even if you have to learn it on your own. Your college might not offer a course to help you develop your "people skills," but if it does, the course is probably titled something like "Human Relations" (as in "I can relate to humans") or "Interpersonal Communications." A good course promotes understanding of oneself and empathy for others as a basis for establishing satisfactory relationships on the job and in everyday living. It also covers listening skills and group decision-making processes. If your college offers such a course, take it—maybe even twice.

Marketing Course

Every business has a marketing plan. Artists who make a living selling their art have to use marketing principles. Performers and athletes market themselves like products.

▶ **HOT TIP**

daytimer.com has some free time management resources.

A study by AT&T showed that about seven years down the road, the more generally educated worker tends to catch up and pass—both in pay and responsibility—the worker with only technical training.

▶ **HOT TIP**

Great on-line article about time management at franklinquest.com/organizational/ knowledge/lib/first.html

Colleges are marketed to high-school students and parents. Churches have fundraising drives that are based on marketing. NBA basketball teams are marketed to the public. Everywhere you go in your work, marketing will be a part of the picture. If you take a marketing course, you'll have a fundamental understanding of a subject that everyone will at some time be involved in. It also looks great on your resume. Most courses will cover marketing environment, segmentation, marketing mix, marketing opportunities, and buyer behavior.

Language Course

Many major companies are doing business globally and they look for employees who can speak another language—or who have taken language classes. It shows an interest and ability to learn new languages. Even if you'll only work in the United States, learn a second language. Research trends point to a very near future where speaking a second language will be a necessary skill.

Take the courses above and you'll have more than an interesting library in your head on the day you graduate. You'll have the business basics that most employers require. Best of all, you'll have the know-how that will enable you to accomplish your dreams.

Making College Work for You

As you may have already experienced firsthand, the way a school teaches may not always be the best way for you to learn. For some people college is an easy way to learn because it matches their learning style. But for many people, listening and reading are terribly difficult ways to learn—like trying to eat rice with a toothpick.

Learning-style specialist Renee Mollan-Masters, author of the book *You Are Smarter Than You Think!*, put it this way:

> *Inside I knew I was smart, but I was never able to perform well in school. In high school I would study the same way my friends were studying except that I would put in considerably more hours and they would get the A's and I would get the C's. This seemed unfair and confusing because, after all, I had put in more time. Learning changed for me when I began studying Speech Pathology. I was learning almost instantly. I graduated with honors. Even years later I was still unaware of what had caused this sudden change in my intellectual ability.*

Renee soon realized what made all the difference—for her to really learn something, not just memorize it for a short while, she had to discover and rely on her particular learning strengths. Listening to a lecture wasn't enough.

You've just been told about a book that could be your key to making college work for you. (I recommend that you read Renee's book and determine *your* personal learning style.) Next you'll learn about a class which enabled a student to quit a job he didn't like and freelance for $25/hr.

▶ **HOT TIP**

Read Joe Girard's *How to Sell Yourself* (Warner).

According to the latest official figures, 43.28% of all statistics are totally useless.

Mike Waters

CHAPTER 12

More, Better, Faster, Digital

Never put off for tomorrow what you can get your computer to do today. As my good friend Leland Russell says, "When I see someone avoiding computers, it reminds me of the caterpillar who saw the butterfly go by and said 'You'll never get me up in one of those things.'" Computers provide an incredible way to learn quickly, act effectively, and get paid well. And no matter what your professional aspirations, computers are going to be involved and there are programs that will make your work easier and of higher quality. Those who do use computers will be rewarded, promoted, and far more successful. We're living in a time when virtually all jobs will require computer skills.

Numerous people have made a lot of money simply because they can use a computer. David Eggers, editor of *Might,* whose story I told earlier, was glad he picked up computer skills during college. Right after graduating he applied for an associate art director job which he didn't get. So he took a nonpaying internship with a newspaper and in order to pay the bills, he used his computer skills to do freelance work. He had intended to work for a newspaper, but his computer skills were paying off so nicely that he used them to launch his own business instead. How much were his computer skills worth? An average of $50/hr.

If you have computer skills, high-paying jobs are everywhere. Temporary services pay their highest wages to people who use computers. Web page designers and desktop publishers often get paid at least $50–$100/hr! There are even video game testing jobs for people with computer skills. Can you imagine getting paid $20/hr to play video games because you have basic computer skills? I'm not talking about computer programming ability here—just the ability to use software.

We are minutes away from software testing in every company. You can no longer hide computer incompetence because it's a computer dominant world.

Marilyn Kennedy

▶ **HOT TIP**

Pick up these three skills and you'll be welcome in the world of internet companies: (1) Get systems experience. (2) Learn to set up a computer or install software. (3) Learn to program in C++.

How to get started with computers

The four most valuable computer skills an employee can have for any business or organization are word processing abilities, an understanding of databases, knowledge of spreadsheets, and Web design skills. If you know how to make your way around these four skills, you will meet with more opportunities. You can learn these four basic computer programs by taking introductory computer classes, attending off-campus seminars, or by learning on your own.

In addition to the awesome access to people and information that computer networks provide, there are numerous ways in which computers can provide you with more POWER TO GET THINGS DONE.

Enhance Your Hobbies

No matter what your hobbies, interests, or career aspirations, computers can help you do more, better, faster, and easier. Many computer programs have been written to assist you in your special interests or hobbies. Whether your interests are astronomy, drawing, astrology, genealogy, music, sports, coin collecting, etc., there is probably a computer program designed especially to help you enjoy and excel at your hobby.

▶ **HOT TIP**

Don't leave college without knowing how to use Microsoft Word, Excel, Access, and PowerPoint (WordPerfect is an application of the past).

▶ **HOT TIP**

There are student centers on the Web. They are loaded with resume examples, cover letter samples, personality tests, and career advisors. You need to check them out. Start with a few I like:
hiredmag.com
careerplanit.com

I am a happy nerd in cyberspace, where no one can see my haircut.

Dave Barry, humorist

Copyright by Kirk Anderson. Used by permission.

THOUGH HE WAS STRANDED ON A DESERT ISLAND, THROUGH MODERN TECHNOLOGY TED STILL PULLED IN $82,000 BEFORE TAXES.

The people have to be able to read and use a computer or we don't have a job for them.
   Gordon Moore, Chairman of Intel

Get Organized and Save Time

Day planning software enables you to get organized, save time, and accomplish more. These programs have great "to do" list capabilities (finally, you don't have to keep rewriting a new list everyday). They also have calendar functions so that you can organize your schedule. And they have effective ways of organizing all those important bits of information that normally get lost on a scrap of paper.

Launch Your Career and Write Your Resume

There are programs that inventory your skills and produce an outline of your resume. There are programs that make your job search quantum times easier by listing companies and addresses that match what you're looking for. You'll usually find these types of programs in the career center. And, of course, you can access many career sites on the Internet that will help you with every facet of the job search. Many are recommended in the appendix of this book.

Next you're going to learn about a student who made up his own conference and learned one of the skills employers want the most.

CHAPTER 13

Excel-eration Training

Amon Rappaport loves his job because he gets the excitement of lobbying on Capitol Hill and the satisfaction of having an impact on national issues that he cares about. Getting his position as a legislative assistant at the Religious Action Center in Washington D.C., was no small feat: He was competing with about 70 cream-of-the-crop candidates from the best colleges in the country.

> *I was an international relations major at Pomona College. During my senior year, I organized a team of students and created a three-day leadership conference that attracted over 150 students from 15 countries across the globe. It was called The World Youth Action Conference. I remember my original idea was to bring students together to discuss global problems, and then my friend Carol said, "Amon that's truly great—bringing students together—but why don't we talk about solutions instead." That's when the concept "How to be effective in social action" was developed.*

You have to go back to the beginning of Amon's college years to understand how he got to the point where he could even seriously consider creating his own conference.

> *I was in a notoriously boring international relations class my freshman year, and I was thinking about the letters I owed to several friends abroad. I got to thinking that I could save myself some writing if I could just get all these people to write to each other.*

Amon posted a flyer across his campus that said, "Find Out What World Youth Think—Let's make a newsletter together."

Ultimately, staying inspired means the most to my happiness. If I were to think in terms of "What will people think of my career choice?" I'd get caught up in a life that is structured by other people's conceptions of what I should be.
Amon Rappaport, legislative assistant at the Religious Action Center

I got three or four people interested (a couple of whom I knew) and we made up a form letter, sending it out to every friend and friend of a friend we could think of. Within a few months, a couple people sent us back articles. We formatted it on a computer, Xeroxed it, and sent it. It really wasn't a tremendous effort, but all of a sudden we were publishing the World Youth Network newsletter. After a few years, the idea of getting our "World Youth" together for a conference came naturally.

Amon thinks back on the time when he put together the conference as the experience that really built his leadership skills.

Working on the newsletter, I made quite a few leadership mistakes, but those lessons were invaluable when I was overseeing five committees to make the conference happen. Granted there were days when I was on the verge of giving up, but I'm glad I stuck with it, because in the end it went smoothly, and I got so much out of it. Not least was valuable management experience and tremendous contacts. For instance, there was an exiled rebel leader from the Sudan who'd been imprisoned for orchestrating a campaign to focus attention on the civil war in his country, and there was a young African-American man who was the official U.S. youth delegate of the World Earth Summit Conference. During the final weekend of the conference, I realized that just being able to spend a couple of days with that caliber of people was the highlight. The payoff. Tremendous!

Some students attend conferences. Some organize the conferences themselves. Some read books. Some participate in "ropes courses" and find themselves perched high in a tree, trying to find the courage to walk a wire tightrope, 50 feet above the ground. Although their activities are vastly different, they are all getting leadership training.

In my work as a speaker, I've come to learn that there are a fortunate few students, like the ones in the examples, who are gaining a huge advantage during college by learning exciting, out-of-the-ordinary lessons. Somehow they tap into an entire body of knowledge that isn't mentioned in the typical college education—knowledge about being effective!

Effectiveness is simply the ability to "make something happen." Leaders are usually effective people. Test your

> Making it a cooperative project—that to me was the most valuable lesson I learned about working with people.
>
> *Amon Rappaport*

> I'd say becoming a good leader may come down to something as simple as being a good listener; listening to people's advice about how to be a good leader and listening to the people you're managing and leading.
>
> *Amon Rappaport*

effectiveness knowledge by asking yourself if you can do the following things with confidence:

- formulate a team vision
- run an effective meeting
- get the cooperation of many different people
- organize a staff for effective action
- assess the varying needs of diverse team members
- plan a large activity from start to finish
- delegate effectively
- publicize your cause
- overcome declining morale
- speak publicly
- think through difficult problems
- evaluate risks and make important decisions

If you haven't had experience in the skills above you're not alone—but you are at a disadvantage because some students are gaining a competitive edge by learning the secrets to being effective. Let me explain. College most likely is not going to teach you these skills and the vast majority of students are going to graduate without being able to do them well. But what if you knew how to gain this expertise on your own?

Gain the advantage

If you want the best from your college experience, try a little trick someone taught me so that no matter what college I go to speak at I can always find the best campus resources in less than 45 minutes.

First go straight to the student life office or the counseling center and ask about leadership programs. If your college offers a leadership program, find a way to join it! These programs are an unbelievably great experience, from the things you learn to the way they teach the lessons. Often these programs are conducted on rope courses or wilderness retreats—fun and challenging stuff!

▶ **HOT TIP**
Order leadership videos for the campus club you participate in. For a comprehensive catalog call Medialearning Resource Group, (800) 225-3959. (You can preview the videos first.) medialearning.com

Use what talents you possess: the woods would be very silent if no birds sang there except those that sang best.

Henry Van Dyke

My favorite leadership books:
• *How to Win Friends and Influence People* by Dale Carnegie (Pocket Books)
• *Awaken the Giant Within* by Anthony Robbins (Simon and Schuster)
• *Finding Your Purpose* by Barbara Braham (Crisp Publications)
• *Life 101* by John-Roger and Peter McWilliams (Bantam Books)
• *Six Action Shoes* by Edward de Bono (Penguin Books)
• *Sacred Hoops* by Phil Jackson (Hyperion Books)
• *Leading Out Loud: The Authentic Speaker, the Credible Leader* by Terry Pearce (Jossey-Bass)
• *The Pursuit of Wow* by Tom Peters (Vintage Books)
• *Handbook for the Positive Revolution* by Edward de Bono (Viking Penguin)

At a Glance. Copyright by Michael J. Saporito. Used by permission.

Next pick up a course catalog and start looking for courses that cover topics like:

- planning

- decision making

- leadership

- human relations

- problem solving

- personal development

- time management

These aren't traditional courses, but often you'll find them offered by a special department (i.e., counseling centers, career centers, or extended education courses for returning students). These are courses in effectiveness. They teach you exciting lessons that you can use in your everyday life. (Did I mention that taking them also impresses future employers?)

Last but not least, ask at the career center for the best place on campus to find personal achievement books, audio-cassettes, and videotapes. It's exciting and surprising to find that at almost every college I visit many of the books that changed my life are available for students to check out. Usually these books and tapes are located in the career center, the student activities office, the counseling center, or the main library.

Don't blow leadership courses off!

"Leadership ability" was the number one quality named as "what businesses want" in a survey by the College Review Board. The resources I've recommended will not only increase your productivity after college, but people pay big bucks to learn these lessons ($3,000 is not an unusual amount for a three-day seminar on leadership or personal achievement).

Philosophically speaking

Most students are going to pride themselves on being intelligent or talented. Beware of priding yourself on those two things because, in the words of Calvin Coolidge, "Nothing is more common than unsuccessful people with talent. Unrewarded genius is almost a proverb." Take pride in being able to "make it happen."

The lessons you learn from the activities suggested in this chapter do teach you to excel. Take these lessons, and then combine them with the suggestion that a college student used to help her make an award-winning film during college, despite the fact that her school didn't even teach courses about film production.

What businesses want:
  1. Leadership ability
  2. Computer proficiency
  3. Exceptional people skills
  4. Oral and written communications skills
  5. A demonstrated team attitude
  6. Flexibility
  7. Problem-solving skills and decision-making abilities
  8. Curiosity
  9. Energy
 10. Knowledge of other cultures and languages
     Source: College Review Board

They always say that time changes things, but you actually have to change them yourself.
Andy Warhol, artist

CHAPTER 14

A Major Shortcut

Tiffany Shlain graduated from U.C. Berkeley as a film theory major. Tiffany made films during college even though there were no film production classes taught on her campus. Tiffany made two films during her college career. Her first short film won the Eisner Prize, U.C. Berkeley's highest art award. Her second short film was highly acclaimed at film festivals.

Although many artists feel they have to give up their art after college for a real job, Tiffany didn't agree. After graduating she stepped up her moviemaking and two years later she was finishing her first big film, with a $250,000 budget, and had recently been hired to head up a team to create interactive movies.

> Never be scared to ask. Call people out of the blue. Take people out to lunch. That's how I've learned what I know.
>
> *Tiffany Shlain, filmmaker*

For my first two years of college I mostly just messed around. I used to always say I was a student of life. I got good grades, but to me the most important things were meeting people from different cultures. My situation was sometimes a little bumpy because my father wanted me to be a doctor; he even went so far as to buy me that book The Making of a Woman Surgeon.

My first mentor was a woman professor teaching film theory—she read a paper I had written out loud in class, as an example of a good paper. I had always loved film but I never thought that it would be a viable choice for me.

I called one of the best film schools in the country, N.Y.U., and asked if they had any course offerings besides their graduate program (because I couldn't afford that). They had a summertime film production course so I signed up and put it to my credit card. But the N.Y.U. course didn't start for another year and I wanted to get started right away. I really wanted to talk to someone about the path they took and about the possibilities of making a living making movies. I went to the library to find out filmmakers' names and I found an article about Bay Area women filmmakers. When I called them they were very receptive. One of the articles that I read was about a film company called Pacific Pictures. I called the woman who owned it, I offered my services for free, and I got an internship.

During her senior year in college Tiffany wrote the script for a film she wanted to make entitled *Zoli's Brain*. Because the usual cost of making a full-length film runs easily near a quarter of a million dollars, Tiffany took on three jobs (reader, waitress, and secretary) and hustled to raise investments from people who attended her film showings. None of her investors were friends or family members, but she did manage to raise $70,000 and enlist over 100 volunteers. How did she achieve this?

There was a really talented guy in my filmmaking class at N.Y.U. and he made a great short film. We'd have to personally present our work and he'd go up in front of the class and talk about how bad his film was and by the end of the hour you believed it and hated it. So much about being an artist is believing in yourself enough that other people can believe in you also. And that's how I got all those people to work for free.

I was supposed to be a doctor, but it wasn't my passion. On one hand I knew it was a steady living, respectful and everything, but I just couldn't do it. Ultimately, it was one of the hardest arguments I've ever had with my father. We fought about it for two years. But now that I've established myself, I've come to realize that it wasn't that my dad didn't want me to be an artist, because he's always been proud of me, but he was genuinely concerned about my future and my ability to earn a living.

So did filmmaking come easily to Tiffany?

I didn't have this blessed life. I was a waitress for four years. I got fired from a cocktailing job. It was so embarrassing. Overcoming my technical fears about filmmaking was really hard. But I would never tell anyone about my fears. "Can you do this?" they'd ask. I'd be like, "Sure, no problem!" Then I'd go home, stress out, try and figure out

I live by the rule play hard, work hard or else I wouldn't be able to do anything I'm doing.

Tiffany Shlain

My next-door neighbors are this grunge band and they hang out all the time. I'm like "What did you guys do today?" "Eh, we just hung out. What did you do today?" "Well I've been working for 20 hours."

Tiffany Shlain

how to do it by reading, and then just jump in with my eyes closed.

If you want to excel at something—maybe it's a game, a sport, or a career—there is one method for becoming great that beats all others. The fastest way to excel at something is to BE COACHED BY THE BEST! Because:

- successful people can tell you the shortcuts

- people who have mastered the game can teach you key strategies and moves

- successful people can open doors for you by introducing you to other successful (and important) people and resources

- being around a person who's really good at their job provides you with a crystal-clear picture of the habits and traits you'll need

- a good coach can give you specific advice about your individual strengths and weaknesses

- even your passion and enthusiasm will be strengthened simply by being around someone who lives passionately and enthusiastically

In short, being around someone who's doing or has done things that you admire is fantastically inspiring and incredibly revealing. Asking for help is a key ingredient in winning a "success coach." My first success coach was Deborah Lowe, a professor at San Francisco State University.

I was enrolled in one of Deborah Lowe's classes and, in no time at all, her knowledge and accomplishments impressed me. One day after class I asked her for help on a cover letter I was trying to write. During the process of getting her help, I also won her respect and her willingness to help me reach my career ambitions. For the next two years, I learned what it feels like to have a success coach. (It feels like you've got a top expert on your side.)

In addition to the encouragement and inspiration that cannot be measured, my success coach taught me many things I would not have learned in class. She pounded the importance of internships into my thick and reluctant head. She taught me how to write an outstanding resume. She showed me where to look for work and how to get paid as much as possible. She taught me how to "package" myself to

All glory comes from daring to begin.

Eugene Ware

I think the success came because in my heart I was still always that young kid from Elmira, hustling for work and for something better, and because I always surrounded myself with great people.

Tommy Hilfiger

win whatever job I desired. And on and on. But the one thing I got from her which is perhaps the most difficult benefit to describe is simply that being around a great person rubs off. Without even trying, somehow I'm a little more like the "Deborah Lowe" that I admire so much.

A success coach is . . .

A mentor is anyone who takes the time to teach you about succeeding. Often the coaching process is called "mentoring." But whether you choose to call this person a "mentor" or a "coach," you're looking for someone who has accomplished things that you'd like to accomplish and is kind enough and willing to take some time each week to help you.

The key to getting a coach

- Find someone you admire and ask them for help with your career development.

- Try to become their assistant or helper.

- Invite them to be a guest lecturer in your campus club.

The key to getting a coach is a three-letter word: ASK. Ask the right person, ask for help, ask with conviction, ask until you get what you want. If you ask, you'll receive.

Maybe your success coach is one of your professors. Have you had a professor that you really admired? Maybe it's a professor that you haven't met yet. Ask your friends for recommendations. Maybe it's a staff member in the career center or the student development center, or someone you admire where you work. Maybe it's someone you know who's already in the working world or one of your peers who seems to be really advanced.

Convincing a success coach that you're worthy

As a rule, you have to win a person's respect before they will coach you. There are exceptions to this rule: Career center counselors and student development staff are paid to coach any student who asks, and they offer self-help books which can either be purchased or read on loan. But in cases where the person is not obligated to coach you, you need to make a good impression. How do you do this? Let me put it this

Do not be content merely to recognize greatness in others; take a further step and imitate it. For in the imitation of greatness is greatness itself.
Sherman Finesilver, chief judge U.S. District Court, delivered at the Front Range Community College commencement, May 7, 1989

I had a lot of mentors. I would go to poetry readings looking for a writing mentor and instead of bombarding them with questions I would hand them a prewritten letter that they could read on their way home.
Veronica Chambers, story editor, New York Times Magazine

way: It's hard to say no to someone who demonstrates these qualities:

- admiration, demonstrated by asking for help, complimenting their expertise, and being grateful for their advice

- ambition, demonstrated by expressing your goals and dreams

- follow-through, demonstrated by taking their advice and completing what you said you would

- courtesy, demonstrated by being considerate of their time and by being well mannered

- respect, demonstrated by trusting what they say

Stay worthy

Being "coached" is not always an easy process. To help you succeed, coaches often have to point out your weaknesses or push you to expand your thinking. Rarely are we taught how to take criticism and even if we can, it remains a painful process. This story may help you work well with your coach.

A Zen master was once asked by a professor (who was widely known for his book learning) to explain Zen to him. The master agreed and began by pouring him a cup of tea. But once the cup was full, the master kept pouring and the tea overflowed into a puddle. "Enough!" said the professor. "The cup is already full and now it is overflowing." "Your mind," said the Zen master, "is like this cup—so filled with your own ideas, views, and concepts that there is no room for any new learning."

Rarely will people coach someone who is resistant to suggestions. Suggestions are hard to take because they can make you feel embarrassed, but suggestions are also your fast pass to growth. When being coached, bite your tongue, put your own views and opinions aside, and try out the suggestions of your coach. If after giving them your best try, you decide that the suggestions are not for you, then you can revert to what you believe is best.

Take the shortcut

Now that you know the fastest way to excel at anything, I'm going to tell you about a simple and exciting activity that can change your life in an instant.

▶ **HOT TIP**

Ask your success coach to write you a letter of recommendation when you're applying for a job. And when you ask, dress professionally. You want your letter written with that image in mind.

The first thing is to realize that you cannot achieve ultimate success alone. Luckily, I was able to get the best coach there is, Tom Telez. I couldn't coach myself. So look for the best coach there is.

Carl Lewis, winner of nine Olympic Gold Medals

CHAPTER 15

Life-Changing Reality Checks

One day, somebody suggested to San Francisco State student David Greene that "informational interviewing" might be a way to figure out a good career. After it was explained to David that informational interviewing was just a friendly way to ask a professional some job questions, he called and spoke with a woman at I.B.M. He had gotten the name of the woman through a friend of a friend. His informational interview at I.B.M. went great. Even though he didn't apply for any work, I.B.M. said there might be the possibility of an internship! The woman also told him about a small company named Interactive Records that puts music and multimedia together. That sounded like a dream job, so he called them. Right away they said, "We're not hiring." David replied, "I'm not calling to ask for a job. I am calling because I heard that you are doing cutting-edge work, and I'd just like to learn more about it." He said the right thing and Interactive Records said, "Oh! Well, why don't you come next week and we'll show you around." David went on this informational interview and basically never left. He's now a part owner in the company.

The journey of 10,000 miles begins with a single phone call.

Confucius Bell

You want your dream job to come true faster? Info-interview with someone who's got your dream job. David Greene feels like one informational interview changed his life. It took him from no job to his dream job! During speeches, I ask who in the audience has done an informational interview. A few hands usually go up. The people who have done them usually say one of three things:

"It was great. I learned a lot about the job and about how to get into the field."

"It was great and they offered me a job!"

"I'm glad I did it because I discovered that it's not my dream job after all!"

Informational interviews provide you with two great things: Answers and connections. In person or over the phone, you interview someone about their job: "What is the job really like? How much does it pay? How do people get into this field?" That's basically all there is to informational interviewing. You talk to a working professional and you get "real-world" insights into the job that interests you. Imagine who you could interview if you really aimed high.

Nuts and Bolts to Informational Interviewing

Any time you are interested in a profession, call someone working in the profession, tell them you are a student, and ask them if you can come in for an informational interview. There's no one in the world who you can't try contacting. People like to help students out with job information. I know one student whose dream job was to run a Fortune 500 company, so he called the president of Levi Strauss & Co., asked for an informational interview, and got it!

To find a working professional, go to your college career center or alumni office and ask for a list of people who are working in the field that interests you. Locate alumni, people you've read about, or people your parents know. Then call those people and say something like:

> *Hi, my name is _____ and I'm a student at _____. I got your name from _____. You're in a line of work that I'm interested in and I was hoping that you could help me gain insights into the profession. I'm sure that my questions could be answered in a ten-to-fifteen-minute informational interview.*

Most of the time they will be more than willing to take ten to fifteen minutes to answer your questions. Sometimes they will want to talk over the phone, but often they will invite you to their workplace. When you can, choose that the interview be at their workplace because you'll learn more and make a stronger connection with the person.

Great questions to ask during the interview:

- How did you get into this field?

- What do you do on a daily basis?

- What percentage of your time is spent doing what?

▶ **HOT TIP**

Learn something about the company first and you're more likely to be offered an internship.

▶ **HOT TIP**

Go to career fairs put on by your college. Get information about job opportunities and ask questions.

▶ **HOT TIP**

College librarians often have access to on-line subscription services like Dow-Jones Interactive and the Standard & Poor's Industry Surveys. Great way to get high-dollar information about companies for FREE!

It takes 7 attempts to make an unsolicited business contact. Most people give up after three.
Don Asher, author of the Overnight Job Change Strategy *(Ten Speed Press)*

- What are the skills that are most important for a position in this field?
- What were the keys to your career advancement?
- Why did you decide to work for this company?
- What do you like most about this company?
- How does your company differ from its competitors?
- What do you like and not like about working in this industry?
- How is the economy affecting this industry?
- What are the professional associations related to this industry?
- What would you do differently if you had it to do over?
- What advice would you give to me?

One Caution

Don't mix informational interviewing with job seeking. Employers will grant informational interviews when they firmly trust that you will not hit them up for a job. The minute you begin trying to get a job, the employer is going to feel misled. If you discover a job that you do want to apply for during the interview, wait until the informational interview is over. The next day, call the employer and tell them that the informational interview not only confirmed your interest in the field, but also made you aware of a position that you would like to formally apply for.

Sometimes they may offer you an internship or job. Many people have conducted informational interviews and have done nothing but ask questions and yet have been offered employment. What do you do if they offer you an internship or job? If it sounds good, take it! Suddenly your life changes in an instant!

Go forth and investigate!

Now you know how to get the inside scoop on your dream job. This activity alone can lead to your dream job or connect you to a mentor, because employers are very impressed by students who have the savvy to do this. There's something else that really impresses employers. It's revealed on the next page.

Learn to call strangers fearlessly and you gain one more key to success.

Donald Asher, author of From College to Career: Entry Level Resumes for Any Major *(Ten Speed Press)*

▶ HOT TIP

Newspapers are a good source for learning about jobs, but not in the help wanted ads. Write to people you read about, congratulate them, and ask them for an informational interview.

▶ HOT TIP

Read magazines from the field you're interested in and call someone who was profiled. Mention that you read the article and were very impressed. This is nice flattery.

▶ HOT TIP

According to research about networking, you are only six acquaintances away from a personal connection to anyone in the world. Six calls away from the most incredible informational interview you can imagine! Go for it.

CHAPTER 16

Really Get Into It

Veronica Chambers has loved reading books ever since she was a kid. But because she thought you had to be anointed or chosen to be a writer, her sophomore year at Simon's Rock College was spent pursuing a legal career. Veronica was working at a legal firm and taking prelaw classes until she noticed that a friend of hers who was interning at a magazine "was definitely having a much better time than I was."

Then the question quickly arose: How could she get a similar internship?

It was really hard. I was a sophomore. I didn't have any journalism experience. I hadn't even taken a journalism class! All I could think to do was sit down with the telephone book and call every magazine in New York. "No, no, no, no," was all I heard until I got to the S's and Sassy *magazine. They had just started up and they said, "If you want to work for free, come on down."*

Try your idea and if it doesn't work, come up with the next one. Keep trying and keep trying and eventually something works.

Veronica Chambers

The internship at *Sassy* magazine opened doors for Veronica to do summer and winter internships at the magazines *Seventeen, Life,* and *Essence.* On her second internship at *Seventeen* magazine she wanted to write, but they required previously published articles. She talked a local high-school newspaper into letting her write a few entertainment stories.

You were supposed to be a high schooler to write for the paper but they let me do it after I pointed out that I was only one year older than some of the seniors. When the articles came out I showed them to the editor of Seventeen *and I begged them to let me write. They started me off with tiny assignments but when I saw my first nationally published article I was so psyched, I instantly started a scrapbook!*

Within a short time, Veronica found herself getting assignments to interview celebrities. She remembers her roommates being excited every time they'd take messages "from famous people they thought were very cool." When she got her own monthly column in *Seventeen* magazine, she was still a junior and had yet to take a journalism class. "It was a tiny column called 'Guy Talk,' nothing big, but it was fun and I got paid $250 each month."

Veronica enjoyed a lot of great internship experiences during college.

. . . I tried for many, many more than I got. I tried for a congressional internship—I didn't get it. I tried for a lot of international internships—I didn't get any of them. I tried for a Rotary scholarship—I didn't get it. I applied for fellowships, endowments, and on and on—I never got any of those. You name it, I applied for it and I didn't get it. But I did get a few things. For instance, I applied for a Glamour *College Woman contest and got picked as one of the Top Ten College Women of that year. I got to go to this big event in New York, was featured in the magazine, and met all of these people in the business. And to think, I had seriously thought applying for that contest was a waste of time. When* Glamour *called to tell me I won, I thought they were trying to sell me a subscription, so I said, "Oh I already get the magazine," and I hung up. So even though I didn't get most of the things I applied for, I always recommend students apply for everything.*

Having gotten so much experience in college, Veronica graduated into an assistant entertainment editor position at *Essence* magazine. Then for six months she was a freelance magazine article writer.

I figured out there was a direct proportion between how many pitch letters you sent out and how many responses you got back. Ten pitch letters would get me two assignments . . . I ended up working at Premiere, *but I pitched them repeatedly, repeatedly, and repeatedly! Finally, after a year and 12 letters, I came home to a message on my machine that said, "I liked your ideas . . . Call me. I want to give you a story." That was the greatest feeling.*

Whenever I met an editor or someone I might want to work with, I'd put them on my mailing list and I'd write them a note every couple of months to tell them what I was working on. It's weird because it makes me sound like Attila the Hun but I'm not.

Veronica Chambers

I've tried everything so it just looks like I've had more successes than failures.

Veronica Chambers

I was waiting for someone to say, "Oh Veronica, you're so smart and you're so special, come work at my magazine." But the thing is you don't need to wait for someone to pick you out of a crowd. You can go out there and do your thing and eventually you find your own star and it seems like you've been picked out of a crowd .

Veronica Chambers

By age 23 Veronica Chambers was story editor for the well-known publication *New York Times Magazine* and was on top of her world.

I love what I do. I love the fact that my job is to find great ideas and great writers. And there's a publishing house that is paying me money to write a book. It's fun and you just want more. It's my dream job and it's a great life.

Any secret tips for aspiring writers?

When I wanted to do an article for Seventeen, *I went to the library and got six months' worth of issues and read them all to come up with ideas that they hadn't done before. Then I would write my pitch letter.*

As her tip for aspiring writers demonstrates, Veronica Chambers would qualify herself for jobs by really getting into the subject matter. Reading books and articles is a great starting place to master the subject at hand, but there are many additional ways to really get into your favorite subject.

Here are 17 ways to "really get into" your subject and establish your expertise:

1. Look up articles at the library (photocopy and save everything).

2. Organize all the articles you find in a three-ring binder.

3. Conduct a computer search for articles and bibliography lists.

4. Read the books that have been written by the experts in the field.

5. Do an informational interview with someone who's already an expert.

6. Attend a conference about the subject matter.

7. Take a seminar or workshop that might be offered off campus.

8. Write down your thoughts about the subject and then turn them into handouts.

9. Get involved in computer "forums" about the subject matter. ("Forums" are where people with similar interests chat and share information via computers and modems.)

10. Take a factory tour if you're interested in something that's manufactured.

11. Take a company tour.

12. Subscribe to a subject-related magazine.

13. Take things you learn and try applying them right away.

14. Associate with people in the field (join the professional club they're in).

15. Get a job of any sort that puts you around the experts.

16. Ask your professors questions about the subject.

17. Talk about the subject with your friends—it's good practice.

There is one extremely hot way to Really Get Into It. This will also massively up your expertise: trade journals. If you get into trade journals while you're still in college you'll be way ahead of the job-seeking pack. Most people don't discover them until two to three years out of college. One of the best things about trade journals is that they're free. All you have to do is correctly fill out the bingo cards in a trade journal that interests you and you're all set. I have personally subscribed to trade journals and they keep you up to date on industry trends, the important companies and products in the industry, emerging markets and research, how-to articles, hot fields, salary surveys, top 500 company listings, industry buzzwords, and much much more. Every industry and field has at least one trade journal, and it's usually free to people

> What real filmmakers do is they study films, they study their craft. No matter how much success they encounter, they are always in the process of studying.
>
> *John Singleton, movie director who continues to watch at least one film a day, a practice he equates with taking vitamins*

▶ **HOT TIP**

A lot of trade journal sites are listed at http://dir.yahoo.com/ Business_and_Economy/ Magazines/Trade_Magazines/

who indicate that they work in the field. Once you've identified an industry that interests you, aggressively subscribe to as many trade journals in that field as you can.

Really getting into your favorite subject is your key to building expertise and staying vital because:

- no one will ever teach you better than you can teach yourself

- many professors are "out of touch" with what you need to know for your profession

- employers practically *require* that you've studied the job you're applying for by at least looking up articles

- 50% of what you're being taught today will no longer be true or relevant in five years. (Let me explain what I mean when I say 50% of what you're being taught

They recall automobiles that are defective. I often wonder why they don't recall diplomas that are over 7 years old.

FM 2030, futurist

today will no longer be relevant in five years. Entire fields and disciplines are changing overnight. Think of it this way: Would you like to be operated on by a surgeon who hasn't learned anything new in the last five years?)

The bottom line is that there are two great reasons to really get into your favorite subjects on your own.

1. If you don't, you'll have one foot planted firmly on a banana peel.

2. If you do, employers will gladly hire you.

I already told you about the time that I looked up 50 articles about videoconferencing and was suddenly qualified to be a videoconferencing manager. Then there was the time I "qualified" myself to speak to college students about career development. I went online and retrieved every article from just about every magazine published in America over the last ten years that contained the words "college" and "success." The search cost me about $50 but at the end of the search . . . Whiz-Bang! The computer spit back well over 100 full text articles. Instantly, without leaving my home, I knew a lot about my subject! (Admittedly, I had to read the articles and think about them a bit first.)

Look it up!

- Look up the things that you want to have expertise on.

- Look up articles and books about the career that you aspire to obtain.

- Look up articles about any company that you're applying to work for.

- Look up things that didn't get talked about enough in class.

- Look up burning questions that your professors can't give solid answers to.

- Look up subjects that you find the most interesting.

At the very least researching your interests will leave you with the kind of reward best described by science-fiction author Ray Bradbury:

I know you feel that once you're beyond these walls and you're employed, you won't ever have to think about school again until you roll down the driveway in your Porsche for your class reunion. But the fact is, you have to keep learning all your life or you're not going to be able to compete.

Harvey B. Mackay

Don't hang with losers. Motivate yourself by associating with strivers. You are likely to perform at the level of those around you.

Willye B. White,
Five-time track Olympian

"Socrates!" "Yeah, we know that name." "Hey, look him up. It's under SOW-KRATES." "Oh yeah, here. 'So-crates: The only true wisdom consists of knowing that you know nothing.'" "That's us, dude!"

Dialog from the movie Bill and Ted's Excellent Adventure

If you stuff yourself full of poems, essays, plays, stories, novels, films, comic strips, magazines, music, you automatically explode every morning like Old Faithful. I have never had a dry spell in my life, mainly because I feed myself well, to the point of bursting. I wake early and hear my morning voices leaping around in my head like jumping beans. I get out of bed to trap them before they escape.

It's my knowledge of basketball that is really high. I know every facet of the game, every trick of the trade, every little motivation, every little technique.

Michael Jordan

Next you'll learn a great way to take the information you look up and instantly turn it into a plus—the same way that helped a college student start a national nonprofit organization that is dramatically impacting the American education system.

CHAPTER 17

Show-and-Tell

Wendy Kopp attended Princeton University and majored in public policy because she wanted a major that had a real-world focus. During her senior year, she wrote a senior thesis paper that proposed an innovative and bold idea: Solve the shortage of teachers in underprivileged schools by recruiting outstanding college graduates to teach in them for a few years. That homework assignment turned out to be the starting point for Teach for America, a privately funded, non-profit organization, launched by Wendy, that five years later had recruited and placed over 2,300 teachers into underprivileged schools in ten states.

It would be easy to assume that Wendy Kopp was a perfect student but she explains:

> *I didn't go to tons of classes and the ones that I did go to, I would either sleep through or write down thoughts about what should be happening in my extracurriculars.*

What extracurriculars? It was mostly just one: A campus club called the Foundation for Student Communications. The FSC was a club that published a magazine and put on conferences, and Wendy said she "randomly" got involved in it because:

> *Someone dragged me to the club's open house and they gave me a mailbox, which for some strange reason I felt obliged to keep going in to check.*

In no time at all Wendy went from checking her mailbox to spending 40 and 80 hours a week experiencing something she'll never forget.

I majored in public policy because it's a very real-world focus. It's not just learning a subject area, it's applying knowledge to solve real-world issues.

Wendy Kopp, founder of Teach for America

Flow, that's what was going on. People were just operating at the edge and it was inspiring to be part of a team that was on a mission to take the organization to the next level. It was much more inspiring than sitting in on lectures about abstract things that, in my mind, really had no impact on the present day.

Did she worry she was overfocusing on extracurriculars?

I never questioned it because it's where my interests were. I was just doing what I enjoyed.

She remembers getting the idea for Teach for America at one of the FSC's conferences that brought student leaders and businesspeople from across the country together to learn from each other.

At that time everyone thought that only the government could solve the problem of low-quality education. But I sat at this conference and watched all these different students from different academic majors express enthusiasm for teaching. That's when it hit me: Why not help solve America's education problem by recruiting bright, ambitious college students to be teachers for a few years? And, since I needed a thesis topic, I proposed that.

About the time that Wendy got the Teach for America idea, graduation was fast approaching and she was not exempt from worry about finding a job.

I had been applying for jobs in the spring, but I was totally uninspired by all the things I was applying for, like investment banking, management consulting, and corporate finance, and the only reason I was applying for them is because those were the companies recruiting at Princeton. But along the way I continued to research my idea for Teach for America and I became completely obsessed with the concept as being workable, and finally decided, a couple weeks before turning in my thesis, that I was going to try and create it as a nonprofit organization.

I hated exams. I can't even tell you how much I hated them. I would become terrified before every exam.

Wendy Kopp

I really learned more in extra-curricular activities than from anything else and I totally put very little effort into academics.

Wendy Kopp

My grades were by no means outstanding.

Wendy Kopp

She started by boiling her thesis paper down into a business proposal and then sent it out cold to the CEO's of 30 major companies.

My hope was that a couple of those proposals would land right and get me a seed grant so that I could continue to get by because I had no money.

The day after graduation, Mobil Corp. gave her a seed grant of $26,000 and soon after Union Carbide said that she could use their offices in Manhattan. The rest is history. Wendy went on using her business proposal, the one that started off as a college paper, to raise millions of dollars in private funding.

Consider an interview scenario where two college graduates are trying for the same job at a nonprofit organization that focuses on educational reform. Imagine that the two candidates have exactly the same qualifications, with only one difference: They answer the question "Why do you want to work here?" differently. One candidate replies, "I'm strongly committed to educational reform," and the other says, "I'm very interested in educational reform. If you'd care to see it, I brought along a paper I wrote about educational reform." Which person do you think will make the most impact? Most likely it will be the person who had the paperwork, because in our society, you cannot underestimate the power of the printed word.

In Western culture, people and employers assign more weight, respect, and significance to things they see in print or on paper. What will you have to show after graduation, in print or on paper, that demonstrates your interests and skills to employers? Most students will have only their degree. You can get an edge by gathering, creating, and saving items that show and tell others about your interests and accomplishments and by using these during interviews.

Good show-and-tell items

- Articles you've gathered which are related to the job of your dreams.

- Newsletters, flyers, or brochures that you helped create for a campus club or organization that you were involved in.

I struggled so immensely with writing when I was in high school. I would go through these painful and agonizing experiences learning to write. But it's the best thing I have ever done because writing is 100% of what has enabled me to do what I've done at Teach for America.
Wendy Kopp

I've become completely inspired to have a truly fundamental impact on the education system.
Wendy Kopp

▶ **HOT TIP**

An excellent book on the use of show-and-tell items is *Portfolio Power: The New Way to Showcase All Your Job Skills and Experiences,* by Martin Kimeldorf (Peterson's).

- A binder that contains handouts from important/ applicable classes.

- If you want to be a TV personality, get video clips of yourself doing campus news.

- If you want to be a photographer, create a portfolio of your best photographs.

- If you want to be a computer programmer, write a sample computer program and carry it to the interview on a diskette.

- If you want to be a graphic artist, create sample brochures and business cards, and organize them into a portfolio.

- If you want to be a historian, write a paper about history and attach some great photos, maps, or interviews. (Better yet, turn your ideas into an interactive computer program.)

- If you want to be a journalist, write articles for your campus newspaper and save them all.

- If you want to be an author, put together a book proposal or write some sample chapters.

- If you want to be a teacher, create a great lesson plan.

- If you want to work at a particular company, gather news articles that are about that company.

The list above isn't all-inclusive, so think of other show-and-tell items that might be perfect for you. Just remember that the point is to gather or create items that are visible signs of your education, enthusiasm, creativity, and productivity.

Two show-and-tell items went a long way toward helping me get selected out of 120 people for a public relations internship at Levi Strauss & Co. I took in eight articles that I had looked up on the company and promotional materials that I had made to promote a rock 'n' roll band that I managed part time. I should point out right away that the employer didn't take much time to look at any of the things I had brought in, but I was later told that they had made a strong impression. Think about it. When I said that I liked the company, I had articles to indicate that this was the truth. When I said that I was interested in public relations and promotions, I had the rock band's promotional materials to make it obvious.

How to present a show-and-tell item

Since bringing samples of your work is much like the child-hood game of show and tell, it is very important to remember that the game is not just show. You need to tell about what you've brought in as well. You can't expect the show-and-tell item to do the talking for you. Bring your strongest work to the interview and when the interviewer is asking about your abilities, extracurricular experiences, or interests, tell your story and briefly offer the show-and-tell item as a visual example. Make this brief so that the employer doesn't think that you're trying to avoid speaking for yourself. If they want to take time to look at your work, go along with it. If they don't seem to want to look at the item, that's OK too. Don't push it, and confidently continue the interview knowing that it's good that they saw what you were talking about.

Lastly

Don't graduate from college without any visible signs of your education, enthusiasm, creativity, and productivity. If Wendy Kopp hadn't written down her ideas for Teach for America, it's highly unlikely that anyone would have taken the concept seriously.

There's one place in particular where you'll find great show-and-tell items, a place that most students never even think of. In fact, one college student found out about it almost by accident, but it resulted in some amazing networking.

CHAPTER 18

Going Pro

Gilman Louie's success story is legendary in the software industry:

19 YEAR OLD COLLEGE STUDENT STARTS A COMPUTER GAME COMPANY ON HIS PARENTS' KITCHEN TABLE.

To back their son's dream, Gilman's parents took out a $60,000 second mortgage on their home. Over a year passed and the company hadn't sold its first product. Friends and relatives started saying to Gilman, "When are you going to stop playing these stupid games and do something serious?" However, by the time he was 26, nobody thought he should stop playing games because he was now the CEO of a $12 million company which gave America computer games like Tetris, Falcon, and Vette! By the time he was 33, the guy who every morning around 10 A.M. searched his pocket for enough change to get a grape soda and M&M's had expanded his company, Spectrum Holobyte, into a publicly owned, international, $60 million corporation.

Gilman went to San Francisco State University and majored in business administration. When asked if he participated in any professional associations during college, without a second's delay, he raised his hand displaying two fingers.

I was in Delta Sigma Pi, a professional business coed fraternity, and DPMA, the Data Processing Management Association. The business fraternity was a great opportunity to network—as a matter of fact, I'm still in touch with the friends and business contacts that I made through it. It also taught me how to deal professionally with people on a social and business level and that was very helpful. The other association, DPMA, focused me on issues that

▶ **HOT TIP**

Join a professional association and list it on your resume. Employers will be impressed because it's likely that they're a member of the association also. Plus, 99% of the other students applying won't even know professional associations exist.

directly related to my company—and equally important, it helped me to network with people in the computer software industry. I can't say enough about the helpfulness of both.

When you become active in a professional association, the rubber hits the road. For instance, if you told me that you wanted to become a book writer, I'd ask when you planned to join the American Society of Journalists and Authors, because I know of no better or quicker way to: learn about your profession; network in your chosen field; gather show-and-tell items; stay up-to-date on the latest trends related to your future job; and be able to put an impressive activity on your resume.

What is a professional association?

Imagine a club of historians, a club of film professionals, a club of accountants, or a club of perfume makers. Such clubs exist. There is a professional association for every profession you can imagine. Literally, there are thousands of professional associations nationally and locally that are organized to help those in the field stay up-to-date in their career. They put together reports and newsletters about the profession and industry, as well as holding conferences, meetings, trade shows, seminars, and workshops. They are mostly composed of people who are already working in the field, but often invite students to join them. Usually there is a membership fee for joining and there is often a discounted student rate.

How to find the professional association related to your career:

- look it up in the *Encyclopedia of Associations*
- call and ask a reference librarian in the business books section for help
- call and ask a professional who is working in the field
- ask a staff member at your career center
- search the Internet

How to get the most on a student budget

Conferences are a big part of association benefits, but it's not always possible for a student to afford the costs, as was the

▶ **HOT TIP**

Newsletters are an excellent source of job leads. Online newsletters and listserves can be found at the Directory of Scholarly and Professional E-Conferences-Kovack's List (n2h2.com/KOVACS), and The Liszt (liszt.com). Subscribe and be networked!

▶ **HOT TIP**

The best book for looking up professional associations is *National Trade and Professional Associations of the United States NTPA* (updated annually). Its subject index makes it incredibly easy to navigate. I looked up "Sex" and it named three related associations. Ask for this book at your career center or library.

▶ **HOT TIP**

Professional associations often have Web sites. Two sites to search for your dream job association are: asaeneet.org and Scholarly Societies Project (lib.uwaterloo.ca/society/overview.html).

case for me during college. But you can still get many of the same benefits. Here's how.

- Locate the appropriate contact person for the association. Explain to them that you are a student without enough money to attend the national conference. Ask them for alternate ways to participate or benefit from the association.

- Ask for conference guides, show exhibitor lists (companies to work for), speaker lists (who's who), and topics covered (what's interesting in the industry).

- Ask if you could get a list of the companies that attended last year's conference; this will give you an idea of what companies are out there.

- Ask if it is possible to get an audiocassette of a workshop that covers how to get into the field. Usually workshops and lectures are taped and available for sale to those who couldn't attend. Maybe they'll give you a tape for free or at a discount because you're a student.

- Tell them that you're trying to learn about the field and its trends and requirements and that you'd appreciate receiving any handouts or information that they could mail you.

- Ask them what conferences are being held closest to your area over the next year.

- Ask them if they need volunteers for any of their events in your area. Maybe this will get you into an event that normally you couldn't have afforded.

Hidden treasure

The most important thing you should have learned from this chapter is this: PROFESSIONAL ASSOCIATIONS ARE OUT THERE AND THEY ARE LOADED WITH RESOURCES THAT WILL JUMP-START YOUR DREAM JOB. Maybe you can't afford the membership fees that they require but still, without a doubt, somebody who's a part of this association can help you get valuable information or handouts for free.

> I'm a great believer in luck, and I find the harder I work the more I have of it.
>
> *Thomas Jefferson,*
> *third U.S. president*

> Chance is always powerful. Let your hook be always cast; in the pool where you least expect it, there will be a fish.
>
> *Ovid (B.C. 43–18 A.D.)*

I attended the National Speakers Association's annual conference and it was an incredible experience. Imagine not knowing a lot about your dream job and then being able to attend one conference where people from all over the country, who have your dream job, are gathering to share information. Imagine getting to sit in on conference workshops with titles like "How to Land a Job in This Field," "How to Excel in This Field," "Changing Trends in This Field." You can get any and every question you ever had about the field answered in one day. Hundreds of companies are represented by people you can meet. It's very likely that you'd meet your next success coach or locate an exciting internship.

Do yourself a big favor by joining, participating in, or becoming acquainted with the professional association that is related to your dream career. In one fell swoop you'll have access to cutting-edge information on how to excel at your work, you'll network with companies and professionals from all over the world, and you'll have a great addition to your resume.

▶ **HOT TIP**

Studies found that people who did 45 to 60 minutes daily of intrinsically valuable, non-competitive activities like meditating or running were more empathetic, better listeners.
William Glasser, author of Positive Addiction *(HarperCollins)*

Professional Association Chart

Let no fears stop you. Go for a very cool and unusual job. There are an almost infinite amount of cool jobs out there and a professional association for each one of them. The chart below is just a SAMPLING of the associations that exist. Remember, there's probably also a magazine or trade journal for each of the careers below that you could be subscribing to.

PROFESSION	PROFESSIONAL ASSOCIATION (OR OTHER MAJOR RESOURCE)	CONTACT
Album promoter	Recording Industry Association of America	riaa.com
Animal trainer	Animal Behavior Society	cisab.indiana.edu
Art director for movies	Society of Motion Picture & Television Art Directors	artdirectors.org
Bicycle designer	USCF Mechanics Program	usacycling.org/ membership/ ?support/ mechanics.html
Bicycle messenger	International Federation of Bike Messengers	messengers.org
Billboard maker	Outdoor Advertising Association of America	oaaa.org
Book buyer or promoter	American Booksellers Association	bookweb.org
Brewmaster	Association of Brewers	aob.org
Business consultant	Institute of Management Consultants	imcusa.org
Cameraperson on a talk show	American Society of Cinematographers	(323) 969-4333

Candy maker	National Confectioners Association	candyusa.org
Carpenter	United Brotherhood of Carpenters and Joiners of America	(202) 546-6206
Cartoon voice specialist	American Federation of Television and Radio Artists	aftra.org
Celebrity interviewer	American Society of Journalists and Authors	asja.org
Celebrity publicist	Public Relations Society of America	prsa.org
Chef	American Culinary Federation	acfchefs.org
Children's book illustrator	Society of Children's Book Writers	(323) 782-1010
Clothing designer	Industrial Designers Society of America	idsa.org
Comic illustrator	Society of Illustrators	societyillustrators.org
Corporate video director	International Assoc. of Business Communicators	iabc.com
Costume designer for movies	Costume Designers Guild	costumedesignersguild.com
Demolition contractor	National Association of Demolition Contractors	Doyleston, PA
Dolphin trainer	American Association of Zoo Keepers	aazk.org
Ecology protector	Nature Conservancy	tnc.org
Event planner	Meeting Professionals International	mpiweb.org
Farmer	United Farm Workers of America	ufw.org
Fast-food restaurant owner	International Franchise Association	franchise.org
Film promoter	Motion Picture Association of America	mpaa.org
Fitness center director	American Fitness Professionals	afpafitness.com
Forester	Society of American Foresters	safnet.org
Ghosthunter	American Society of Psychical Research	aspr.com
Greeting card writer	Greeting Card Association	greetingcard.org
Handwriting analyst	American Association of Handwriting Analysts	handwriting.org/aaha/aahamain.htm
Historian	American Historical Association	theaha.org
Holistic medicine expert	American Holistic Medicine Medical Association	holisticmedicine.org
Horse Trainer American	Quarter Horse Association	aqha.com
Hypnotherapist	National Guild of Hypnotists	ngh.net
Interior decorator	American Society of Interior Designers	asid.org
Joke writer for comedy TV show	American Guild of Variety Artists	http://home.earthlink.net/~agvala/agva1.html
Laser tag business owner	International Laser Tag Association	lasertag.org
Leadership trainer	American Society for Training and Development	astd.org
Magazine article writer	American Society of Journalists and Authors	asja.org
Magazine editor	Magazine Publishers of America	magazine.org
Magician	Society of American Magicians	magicsam.com
Massage therapist	Associated Bodywork and Massage Professionals	abmp.com
Mathematician	American Mathematical Society	ams.org

Movie critic	On-line Film Critics Society	ofcs.org
Multimedia artist	Multimedia Development Group	mdg.org
Museum curator	Independent Curators Inc.	(212) 254-8200
Music recording engineer	American Federation of Musicians	afm.org
Newsletter publisher	Direct Marketing Association	the-dma.org
Park designer	American Society of Landscape Architects	asla.org
Performer at colleges	National Association of Campus Activities	naca.org
Photo editor of magazine	American Society of Picture Professionals	aspp.com
Private investigator	Private Eye International	pi-international.com
Product packing designer	American Institute of Graphic Arts	aiga.org
Professional speaker	National Speakers Association	nsaspeaker.org
Radio reporter/ station manager	National Association of Broadcasters	nab.org
Rodeo clown	Rodeo Clowns and Bullfighters Association	(800) 687-4122
Scriptwriter for TV, film, or corporate video	Writers Guild of America	wga.org
Stage manager	Theater Communications Group	tcg.org
Stuntman	Stuntmen's Association of Motion Pictures	stuntmen.com
Stuntwoman	Stuntwomen's Association of Motion Pictures	stuntwomen.com
Talent coordinator for talk shows	National Association of Broadcasters	nab.org
Teacher or educator	American Association for Employment & Education	aaee.org
Theater arts person	Art Search	(212) 697-5230
Theme park ride designer	Int'l Association of Amusement Parks & Attractions	iaapa.org
Toy manufacturer	Toy Manufacturers of America	toy-tma.org
Travel or food writer	International Food, Wine & Travel Writers Assoc.	ifwtwa.org
TV weathercaster	American Meteorological Society	ametsoc.org/AMS
Wilderness challenge course leader	National Society for Internships and Experiential Education	nsee.org

You probably won't find the professional association you're looking for on the chart above because it's just a small sample of associations. You'll have to look up the professional association that matches your dream job on your own (unless you're lucky enough to have spotted exactly what you were looking for on this short sample list).

Break Time

Still reading this book? Good for you! You're demonstrating persistence.

Nothing takes the place of persistence. Talent will not. Nothing is more common than unsuccessful people with talent. Genius will not. Unrewarded genius is almost a proverb. Education will not. The world is full of educated derelicts. Persistence alone has solved and always will solve the problems of the human race.

Calvin Coolidge

Persisting to the next section of this book is very important. You've come a long way with the discovery of your interests and of activities that build your expertise and professionalism. If you're doing the things suggested in this book, you're going to get lucky. Maybe you'll get lucky with a really great job or acceptance into a great graduate program. But you can't do the things in this book and not get lucky because luck favors the one who works hard, prepares, and pursues his or her dream. So:

- you will be the person working the hardest if you've read this book and followed through on many of its suggestions

- your mind will be prepared if you've participated in campus clubs, learned from a mentor, looked up information about your interests, or taken leadership classes

- you will be the person going after your dream if you've tapped into your interests and decided the best ways to pursue them

In the Next Chapters You'll Learn:

- how to practically get a guarantee on a great job after college

- how to walk into any interview with the odds stacked in your favor

- how to plan out shortcuts

- how to decide what the next step will be that affects the rest of your life

Now for the best job-getting suggestion you'll find in this entire book according to recent college graduates. And it's the same suggestion that got Tabitha Soren a job on MTV.

CHAPTER 19

School Without an Internship Can Get You Nowhere

Tabitha Soren is a young journalist who's been on television a lot. Maybe you know Tabitha from MTV, where she hosted MTV's hourly news reports and cohosted *The Week in Rock* with Kurt Loder. Or maybe you remember her as the young news reporter interviewing President Bill Clinton and President George Bush for MTV's "Choose or Lose" election '92 coverage. Or maybe you know Tabitha from *NBC Nightly News* where she was a contributing correspondent. Or maybe you read her twice monthly column in the *New York Times*. Where was Tabitha before all this notoriety and how did she get so lucky?

First of all, Tabitha Soren went to college and geared everything in her life towards getting a job as a reporter, the job she had dreamed about doing since she was in junior high school.

> *I got involved in the campus radio station and newspaper from day one. I was aware that the Key Club and the French Club were sort of inane for what I wanted to do—they were not geared toward getting me a job and, at that point in my life, I chose to gear everything I was doing towards getting a job as a reporter.*

Next she did an internship at CNN at the end of her freshman year. CNN was a typical internship: a nonpaying mixture of exciting and not-so-exciting work.

> *On the downside, I answered phones, did Xeroxing, and always got my hands all black and icky from having to go through newspapers and clip out every entertainment arti-*

I am good reporter because of the sum of all my parts. I'm no beauty. I'm no Pulitzer Prize–winning writer. I'm no Oscar-winning director. But my combined skills make me a good asset to a news organization.
Tabitha Soren, MTV news anchor

Because of my age and because I'm a female, I'm constantly dealing with ageism and sexism and this raised eyebrow but you can't let it get to you if it's something that you believe in. I can get frustrated afterwards, but I try not to let it get to me during the process.
Tabitha Soren

105

cle there was. I also learned some hard lessons. Bill Graham, the concert promoter, was going to be a guest on our show. I was so excited to be meeting him because he was a giant in the history of rock 'n' roll and I knew tons about him. I picked him up in a limo, brought him back to CNN, and I sat him down on this couch in the executive producer's office. I just sort of left him there waiting for the show to start and I was going to bring him into makeup when the time came. Well, when the time came to get him, he was furious and he was walking out! The office went into a huge crisis! People were trying to convince Bill Graham to stay and he was yelling things like "You guys treated me like cattle. You didn't even offer me coffee!" I was flipping out thinking, "This is my fault. The guest is walking out because I didn't treat him well enough." Luckily, the producers rode the elevator down with him and convinced him to stay, so he rode the elevator back up and did the interview. But through the whole interview he was grumpy and I was mortified!

Despite the unpleasantness of the lesson she learned with Bill Graham and despite some of the inane tasks she and the other interns had to do, Tabitha raves about the experience overall.

I learned tons and tons. I ended up covering stories on occasion with a news crew and gaining responsibility for getting a weekly entertainment listing created and on the air. It was definitely a great internship. It prepared me to be hired as a production assistant at MTV. It doesn't have one high point because each time I did something well they let me do something better.

At the end of the CNN summer experience, one of the CNN executives recommended her to MTV. She did part-time work for MTV during her sophomore year in college at New York University, and that made getting a job at MTV after college as simple as a phone call to a previous boss.

During college I started as a production assistant on a show called "Year in Rock 1986." I did the job for four months—pulled tapes for producers, transcribed interview tapes. It was basic tedious work. But, I was excited to be

> I didn't know exactly where I wanted to go to school but I knew I wanted to be in New York City because I figured there would be a lot less competition for internships—a plethora of opportunity for slave labor.
>
> *Tabitha Soren*

> Somehow it had been instilled in me that it was very difficult to get a job, especially in the field I wanted to enter, but that if you worked hard enough, anything was possible.
>
> *Tabitha Soren*

> Most of my journalism classes were duplicating what I had already learned in my internships. I cruised through those classes. I wish I had taken more classes that had nothing to do with journalism. It was stupid to pay all that money to be taught stuff I already knew.
>
> *Tabitha Soren*

there. It was MTV, the show I had been watching since I was 13! (And there were lots of cute, long-haired, frustrated musicians working there so it was good for my hormones.)

After four months Tabitha's work on the project was complete, but she secured more part-time work by doing fill-in writing for people when they were sick and by pitching in on extra-busy days. She was doing her dream work: reporting rock 'n' roll news.

We'd have a meeting in the morning saying, "Rod Stewart got arrested, Eddie Van Halen is in rehab, YES is going out on tour. Michael, you do the Eddie story. Tabitha, you do Rod Stewart." I'd call their publicist to find out what happened, get a photo of them, see if I could get any videotape regarding the issue, and write it up for one of the VJs to read.

In addition to her ability to write (which she had polished while reporting for the college radio station and campus newspaper), something else made 19-year-old Tabitha Soren valuable at MTV.

They were impressed with my knowledge of stupid music trivia. I've been obsessed with music since I was a kid. I have so much trivial, inane knowledge in my head—even back then I could name all the members of Yes, I knew Patti Smith's birthday—little stuff like that actually came in handy at MTV. My brain just retains that kind of information for some reason. I wish it would retain more about history or calculus, but instead, I know REO Speedwagon's bass player's daughter's name!

Tabitha loved working at MTV part time, but she eventually stopped because her real dream was to be an on-air television reporter, and there was no such opportunity at MTV. She paid her dues doing desk assistant work at *World News Tonight* with Peter Jennings, and WNBC, and then after graduating in 1989, she went looking for her big chance. She got it within a month as an on-air reporter and anchor of the eleven o'clock news, at an ABC station in Vermont.

It was at this job that she learned a valuable lesson in life.

When I got the job I packed up everything, left my boyfriend, and moved to Vermont where I had no friends. I

> There would be days when I'd go to school from 9 A.M. till 3, then be a desk assistant at *World News Tonight* from 3 till 7, then change out of my suit and into my jeans and start writing "Head Bangers Ball" for MTV.
>
> *Tabitha Soren*

> During my MTV interview I was asked, "What's your rate?" I had no idea how much people are paid and I was so anxious to have a job that paid that I said "Minimum wage would be fine" and she said, "You're hired!"
>
> *Tabitha Soren*

> Learning interpersonal skills has been more difficult. The things that make you a good reporter don't necessarily make you a good person: aggressive; direct; blunt; hurried. I have to remember that not everyone is on deadline pace and even when I am, I need to treat people well. It's good to remember because life isn't about work, it's about people.
>
> *Tabitha Soren*

guess I thought that by becoming a reporter I would also become a complete person, but it didn't work that way. I realized my boyfriend makes me happy, my friends make me happy, and I found myself unhappy and seriously depressed without them. So I quit the job, moved back to New York, concentrated on my personal life, and that's when everything fell into place. Not to be super-Zen or anything, but as soon as I stopped worrying if I was going to be on 60 Minutes *before I was 30, everything fell into place. It was a good lesson to learn early on.*

The lesson that she learned—that a career alone cannot make a person feel whole—is not the only good she got out of her first job. She also got all the experience she needed to handle herself as a television reporter. And when she got back to New York she called on her old boss and was back to work at MTV. In a short amount of time the inevitable happened; she got her current job as MTV's news anchor.

DON'T EVEN THINK OF NOT DOING AN INTERNSHIP OR CO-OP DURING COLLEGE.

Students who have done an internship or co-op have the edge on jobs. Every other year, the California State University surveys its spring bachelor's and master's graduates regarding their careers. When asked "What is the most important factor in assisting you to find work?" the number one answer was "work experience, volunteering, internship" (56% gave this answer as compared to 13% who answered "academic major" and only 4% who named "above average G.P.A."). Referring to students who have done a co-op or internship, E. Sam Sovilla, assistant vice president for cooperative education at the University of Cincinnati, said, "Their extensive work experiences make them especially attractive to employers."

Consider These Facts

- According to a 1997 study at Northwestern University, 64% of interns are eventually offered jobs with their host employers.

- A 1998 Vault Reports survey found that 77 percent of all college seniors had completed at least one internship by graduation, and 55 percent had participated in two or more.

COLLEGE GRAD

Lunatic Fringe. Copyright by Ward Makielski. Used by permission.

Do as many internships as possible. My friend Marney had six during college. Intern somewhere for a month! Intern anywhere!

David Eggers

- About 40% of co-op graduates will accept a career job offer from one of their co-op employers, according to the College Placement Council.

- U.S. Department of Labor estimates that 48% of all job connections are made through personal networking. Internships and co-ops are a great way to network.

A few people who did internships:
Connie Chung
Bill Clinton
Nancy Collins
Patrick Ewing
Calvin Klein
Spike Lee
David Letterman
Tabitha Soren
George Stephanopolous
Oprah Winfrey

Instead of rejecting your resume because it only shows academic experience, employers will take comfort in seeing that you have real-world work experience already under your belt. While you're getting a great first job, friends who didn't do a co-op or internship will be flipping burgers.

Internships Are . . .

Internships are part-time jobs in the real world that are related to your academic and career interests. They typically last three to six months. The only time an internship might be full time is over the summer when students are usually not in school. For a student, it's an opportunity to get work experience in the real world and academic credit. For an employer, it's an opportunity to get cheap entry-level help and a chance to help students grow professionally.

Most internships don't pay wages at all. Some internships pay a little. But all internships pay off in the near future. My

▶ **HOT TIP**

If you can't find an internship you're interested in, remember that any internship will move you closer to your dream job.

first internship with a small company paid nothing. My second internship with a large and prestigious company paid $6/hr. and then turned into a $25/hr. job after graduation.

Co-ops Are . . .

Co-ops are much like internships, except that they pay a salary and typically last over a year. Most co-op programs offer you academic credit for doing the work, and, on average, the typical student makes $7,500 annually. Also, co-ops are usually available to sophomores and freshmen at two-year schools, while internships typically are available to upperclassmen. (In case you were wondering, co-op stands for cooperative education, meaning that the employer and school cooperate.)

How to get an internship

There are quite a few ways to go about getting an internship, but the most helpful factors are some campus club experience and a bit of persistence. Tabitha Soren went through a lot to get her internship at CNN.

> *I applied to a gazillion newspapers for internships and got turned down for all of them because I was only a freshman, at least that's what they said, so I asked one of my professors if he could help me and he gave me a contact at CNN. At the interview I had clips, articles I'd written for the campus paper, to demonstrate my journalism experience.*

Below are seven possible ways to find internships:

1. Ask at your campus career center.

2. Contact the office designated to coordinate cooperative education.

3. Ask the academic department chairperson of your major.

4. Call your campus alumni and ask if there are internships at their companies.

5. Call your favorite company and ask if they have an internship program.

▶ **HOT TIP**

Get a written job description for your internship or co-op and save it because you can use that job description to describe the internship on your resume.

▶ **HOT TIP**

Internships at higher executive levels are better. Higher level people have more ability to get you a permanent position, create a job, or find someone else who would want to hire you.

6. Log on and look for internships on the net. Check out these two sites for starters:
www.careerplanit.com
They list internship and co-op opportunities around the country. Plus it's a site loaded with on-line advisers.
www.internjobs.com
This site lets you search for internships all over the country and the world. It will let you search by location or key word. There are hundreds of internships listed.

7. Consult these books (check your career center or library for them):

The Back Door Guide to Short-Term Job Adventures by Michael Landes. Published by Ten Speed Press, 1-800-841-2665. This book contains over 40,000 listings of unique internships, seasonal work, volunteer opportunities, overseas jobs, and short-term adventure jobs. www.backdoorjobs.com

Peterson's Internships. It lists over 40,000 internships all across the country. Call 1-800-338-3282 if it's not available on your campus.

The Internship Bible by Mark Oldman and Samer Hamadeh. Published by the Princeton Review, 1-212-874-8282. Lists over 100,000 internships.

An alternative option

If for some reason you don't do an internship or co-op, work for a temporary employment agency during your summer break. Organizations always need temporary workers to do various kinds of entry-level work. You can get temp jobs by looking under Employment Agencies in the yellow pages and calling for a few appointments. Once you start working for an agency, they will start sending you out on jobs that last typically between one and five days, but occasionally even longer.

On top of temporary work providing you with fairly steady summer employment, it is not unusual for temps to get offered permanent work once they've proven themselves on the job. And like co-ops, you gain practical work experience, you get to work in a variety of environments, you enhance your skills, and you get paid. Much better experience for your resume than working as a waitress or waiter.

Large and small firms are beginning to view internships as a recruiting tool, letting interns "try out" for three months to a year.
Roberta Carver, internship coordinator at Emory University in Atlanta

▶ **HOT TIP**

Arrange your schedule to have blocks of time to accommodate a part-time job of 10 to 20 hours per week. Students with the most available weekday time have an edge on getting the job.

▶ **HOT TIP**

Start your career working for a company with less than 250 people, because in a small company you can figure out every part of what the company does.

▶ **HOT TIP**

Monitor your learning curve, not your earning curve.

▶ **HOT TIP**

The Experienced Hand: A Student Manual for Making the Most of an Internship. To order, call the National Society for Experiential Education, (919) 787-3263. nsee.org

▶ **HOT TIP**

While you're doing an internship, look for salaried-position opportunities; check the company bulletin boards; ask the personnel department. While you're working at the company, you've got a better chance.

One last thing

You're doing an internship to gain valuable experience. You can expect to do a lot of clerical work mixed in with some higher level tasks. When you feel that you're not learning much from the internship it's time to ask your superior to increase your responsibilities. If your responsibilities don't get upped, leave the internship for another one. The company that you're interning for will often want to keep you working a long time because you provide inexpensive help for them. Don't be slave labor and don't stay in a dead-end position even if they offer you more money. Gravitate to situations where you'll learn a lot. Learn everything you can and then leave when the learning's done. Keep your learning curve steep and in a few short years you'll be worth more (and earn far more) than if you had stayed in a comfortable, dead-end job.

Once you've found internships or co-ops that you'd like to apply for, you'll be at a point where you need to know exactly how to set things up so that you win the job you want. A lot of people will suggest that you put together a good resume and memorize the answers that are perfect for the "tough" interview questions. I beg to differ. I think the easiest way to win a job is to have the odds stacked in your favor before you even walk in the door. And you can stack the odds in your favor by following a surefire, nine-step, ultra interview plan.

CHAPTER 20

The Surefire, Nine-Step,
Ultra Interview Plan

Harvey B. Mackay, best-selling author and president of Mackay Envelope Corp., tells the true story of a young man who came to interview for a job at his company.

I asked him right off the bat what he had done to prepare for the interview. He said he'd read something about us somewhere and that was about it. Had he called anyone at Mackay Envelope Corporation to find out more about us? No. Had he called anyone who did business with our company? Our suppliers? Our customers? No. Had he checked his university's alumni office to see if there were any graduates working at Mackay he could interview to learn about our corporate culture? Had he asked any students or teachers for their advice? To grill him in a mock interview? To share information? Did he contact the chamber of commerce, go to the library, locate some newspaper clippings on us, or check us out in D&B? If we'd been a publicly held company, which we aren't, could he have gotten his hands on our annual report and any brokerage house recommendations? Did he write us a letter before he came in to tell us about himself, what he's doing to prepare for the interview and why he'd be right for the job? Was that letter a custom-made piece, for us and us only, not an all-purpose flyer? Did it show us his communication skills, his knowledge of our company, his eagerness to join us, and what he had to offer? Was he planning to follow up after the interview, write us another letter indicating his continued high level of interest in the job? Had he planned a way to make sure the letter would be in our hands within 24 hours of the meeting, possibly even hand delivered?

Are you worried about pressure? I look at it this way: Pressure is having to do something you are not totally prepared to do.
Harvey B. Mackay

It will take you no more time to prepare really well for one interview than to wander in half prepared for five. And your prospects for success will be many times better.
Harvey B. Mackay

113

In this case, the answer to every question was the same: NO. This left me with only one other question: The question I never asked because I already knew the answer. How well prepared would this person be if he were to go out and call a prospective customer for us?

It will take you no more time to prepare really well for one interview than to wander in half prepared for five. And your prospects for success will be many times better.

Delivered as an MBA commencement address, Penn State University, May 11, 1991. Courtesy of Harvey B. Mackay and Vital Speeches of the Day

Less than 10% of job offers are generated solely by resumes.

▶ **HOT TIP**

Read the yearly issue of *Planning Job Choices . . . A Valuable Guide to Your Career.* Available through your career center or on-line at jobweb.org/jconline/. There are also special editions for careers in business, science and engineering, and healthcare.

Most people are under the false impression that a resume and cover letter are the keys to winning a job. In actuality, your resume and cover letter are only a small part of what impresses an employer. Here's how to cover all the bases for an interview. I call it the SUREFIRE, NINE-STEP, ULTRA INTERVIEW PLAN and I caution you to use it only when you really, really want to win the job!

This plan wins jobs. But executing the plan takes considerable effort. If you don't want to spend much time preparing I recommend one of two things. Go to the interview dressed nicely, with a resume; skip the interview because you'll probably lose the job to someone who really wants it.

The surefire, nine-step, ultra interview plan

1. Look up articles about the field of interest.

2. Go on an informational interview with someone in a similar position.

3. Investigate the company where you're applying.

4. Write a great resume and cover letter.

5. Bring a show-and-tell item.

6. Dress professionally.

Once you're prepared, you never know what roads will open up. And if you're prepared, it does not matter. If there's a road you can pursue it. If there's no road, you can carve it through bushes.

Jesse Jackson

7. Practice interviewing at your career center.

8. In the interview rely heavily on good human relations principles.

9. Follow up with a thank-you letter sent the same day.

OK, so you really, really want the job and you're willing to put in some extra effort. Here's how to make the plan work for you:

1. Look up articles about the field of interest.

Start by going to the library and looking up articles about the field of interest. This is the starting point because knowledge about the field is very important and articles that you've looked up will help you converse in the interview.

2. Go on an informational interview with someone in a similar position.

When you hit the real interview, you really want to know what the job is all about. If you're going to interview with the director of marketing, go on an informational interview with a different director of marketing. Here's where you ask about what professional associations could help you, what magazines and journals you might benefit from reading, and what things you could highlight on your resume.

3. Investigate the company where you're applying.

If you go to an interview without having investigated the company, you might as well also show up late. Don't get yourself into an embarrassing situation like the student in Harvey B. Mackay's story. Call to find out more about the company. Check with your alumni office to see if you can do an informational interview with any graduates who are already working there. Go to the library and locate some newspaper clippings. Get your hands on the annual report. Find out everything you can about the company before the interview!

4. Write a great resume and cover letter.

There are many aspects to putting together a great resume and cover letter, and I suggest you get custom, professional advice from a counselor at your career center. But I can tell you that a mind-blowing resume would include: Campus club experience, leadership experience, work experience, membership in a professional association, and an internship or co-op. A great cover letter would give two specific examples of how your skills and abilities match the job's description needs.

▶ **HOT TIP**

Don't wear cologne or perfume. Recruiters often mention not liking it. Freshly showered is enough.

I go on my first job interview, and the guy interviewing me is a complete maniac. He goes, "What do you want to be? A disc jockey?" I go, "Yah." And he goes, "What are you? An asshole? Stupid?" And I go, "No, I'm not stupid. In fact, I'm a graduate of Boston University."

Howard Stern

▶ **HOT TIP**

In your cover letters and follow-up letters, don't use overconfident statements like, "I look forward to helping you lead Pacific Industries into the twenty-first century."

5.   Bring a show-and-tell item.

This is a biggie that most people miss. If you create something, you can show it to the interviewer and they'll be able to see that you are creative, productive, and serious about your interests. Maybe it's something you created for your campus club, or a relevant paper you did, or the articles you gathered in step one.

6.   Dress professionally.

Research has confirmed repeatedly that professionally dressed people are always perceived by prospective employers as more intelligent, likable, and credible. As a college student, you probably don't judge people by the way they dress, but you'd be foolish to think that employers won't judge *you* by *your* clothing. You will not get jobs if you are perceived to be dressed unprofessionally or sloppily. You will have a lot in your favor if you are perceived to be dressed right for the job. In other words, forget about your personal style. If you're scheduled for an interview, drop by ahead of time to see how employees dress for important business meetings and copy them. This way you can seem to fit in easily and the interviewer can relate to you.

7.   Practice interviewing at your career center.

A practice interview with a staff member from your school's career center is like a warm-up lap before a big race. It's an opportunity to get feedback on your resume, your outfit, and your answers to those "tough" questions that the employer might ask.

8.   In the interview rely heavily on good human relations principles.

Don Casella, director of San Francisco State University's career center, once gave me a very practical insight about interviewing. He said, "You can't prepare for an interview the way you prepare for a test. You can't try to memorize all the right answers. You have to prepare for it like it's a relationship." I know of no better way to do what Don's suggesting than to rely on timeless gestures of friendliness.

- Smile.

- Take a genuine interest in the other person. Encourage them to talk about their interests and passions by asking questions and listening attentively.

▶ **HOT TIP**

Attention-getting gimmicks aren't usually well received. Gimmicks like pop-up and fold-out multi-colored resumes, homemade videos, helium balloons, attempts at humor, and packages of goodies. Employers see them as too "slick." Better to stick to the Surefire Plan.

▶ **HOT TIP**

Call and request a good sample cover letter and resume from someone who works in a similar position to the one that you're applying for.

▶ **HOT TIP**

Save papers you do during college because if they're well written and applicable to the job you want, they make good show-and-tell items.

▶ **HOT TIP**

If you don't like the person you're going to be working with—don't take the job!

- Look for things you like about the person and compliment them on these qualities.

- Remember the greatest gift you can give a person is treating them in a manner that conveys that you feel that they are valuable.

If you'd like to read about the art of human relations, I cannot recommend any book more strongly than Dale Carnegie's *How to Win Friends and Influence People*. Maybe the title sounds like *Sneaky Methods for Manipulating People*, but I assure you, its advice is not about quick-fix influence techniques or power strategies. It is about basic principles of good relationships and enduring happiness. A more appropriate title might have been *How to Win Genuine Friends and Influence People Respectfully*. It was named by a Library of Congress survey of readers as one of the top ten books that had influenced their lives the most. It is the second best-selling book of all time, surpassed only by the Bible.

9. *Follow up with a thank-you letter sent the same day.*

Following up with a thank-you letter immediately tells the employer that you are professional in your communication and are sincerely interested in getting the job. Also call five to seven days after the interview and remind the employer that you're interested. If you get voice mail or a receptionist leave a simple message: "I just called to tell you that I'm really interested in the job. If you would like to call me, here's my number."

So that's the plan. Follow the Surefire, Nine-Step, Ultra Interview and most employers will react as if you stepped down from a cloud and handed them a golden resume.

The script below is based on the true-life thoughts of a professional job recruiter named Thereza Lewis who hires college students for summer employment. Follow the above nine steps and these could be the thoughts that go through your interviewer's head:

Thereza at the Temporary Service Agency gets your cover letter and resume in the mail. Then comes the time to pick someone for the job.

RECRUITER'S THOUGHTS: *I have hundreds of resumes! Too many to look through. I'm going to toss every one that has a bad*

▶ **HOT TIP**
Before doing a job interview, go get a how-to book for the career you're applying for.

▶ **HOTTEST TIP**
The book *How to Win Friends and Influence People* by Dale Carnegie (Pocket Books).

Do you have any interview tips? Rule No. 1: Just be yourself. Unless, of course, you're sloppy, lazy, or otherwise undesirable, in which case, be someone else. Be ready to humbly sell yourself, and if someone asks about your weak points, say, "Occasionally I just work too hard" or "Occasionally I forget if Fillmore was president before or after Garfield."
*Rainbow Rowell,
the Daily Nebraskan*

Just be yourself, that's the only way it can work.
Johnny Carson's words of advice to Conan O'Brien

Interview Don'ts:

1. Don't walk in with a "know it all," egotistic attitude.
2. Don't exaggerate your qualifications or experience.
3. Don't start off with questions about salary/benefits.
4. Don't come unprepared and offer lame excuses for it.
5. Don't give the impression that you have no career direction.
6. Don't come back with shallow or vague answers.
7. Don't say you have no questions for the interviewer.
8. Don't talk more than you listen.
9. Don't dress in anything other than your professional best.
10. Don't show up without knowledge of the job or the company.

Source: Campus Connections *magazine, published by MarketSource Corp.*

▶ **HOT TIP**

If an association is on your resume, make sure you've attended a function or know what was in the last newsletter.

layout, typo, grammatical error, and a cover letter that's obviously a form letter. [Throw-throw-throw.] Okay—that leaves me with ten and only five of these state the qualifications and objectives I'm looking for. College students are so easy to weed out!*

You were one of the five selected for interviewing. You walk into the recruiter's office ready to interview.

RECRUITER'S THOUGHTS: *Finally someone who actually looks like they're here for an interview instead of a pizza delivery. Professionally dressed and a very nice smile. Now hopefully she didn't pour on the perfume—the last guy's cologne was way too much.*

The interview proceeds and Thereza reviews your resume.

RECRUITER'S THOUGHTS: *Hmmm … a well-balanced education. She's had some volunteer experience where it looks like she got some real work experience, president of a campus club so she's probably a leader and a team player, and she has computer skills.*

From talking with you, Thereza finds out this job is related to your strongest interests and dreams.

RECRUITER'S THOUGHTS: *Good. I wanted someone who really had enthusiasm for the work. Most people don't know what they want but this person seems to.*

As the interview proceeds, Thereza likes the way you smile, listen, and act respectfully. She also likes the way you asked about her award hanging on the wall—it's something she's proud of.

RECRUITER'S THOUGHTS: *I really like this person. I get a really good feeling about her.*

Next you show Thereza the articles about the company that you looked up and mention that you talked to someone in another department.

RECRUITER'S THOUGHTS: *Wow, this person is ambitious and really interested in working at our company.*

Then Thereza discovers that you're a member of the Temporary Recruiters Association.

RECRUITER'S THOUGHTS: *That's the same club I'm in! This person seems so perfect for the job: experienced, ambitious, enthusiastic, professional, confident, self-motivated, and very easy to get along with. This is the person I'm hiring—I'm not even going to interview anyone else.*

Now that you know how to win the job you really want, you're ready to learn a super-simple planning technique that will enable you to achieve your dreams years sooner than you think.

CHAPTER 21

Future-Perfect Planning

For some reason, many of us would prefer to skip paying the long dues that most people believe are required to get a dream job. Are you one of those people? Would you prefer the shortest route to your dream job? What I'm going to teach you is a planning process that dramatically accelerates your success curve. Believe it or not, it is a three-step technique that is taught in advanced business schools like the prestigious Wharton School of Business and in lofty management seminars where I learned it. It goes like this:

1. Picture yourself years down the road and massively successful.

2. From the future-perfect place you're imagining, ask yourself these questions (it does help to also share these questions with a person who might have more specific answers):

   a. What does your business card say on it?

   b. What kinds of books did I read to help myself achieve this success?

   c. What kinds of people do I work with? Are some of them famous?

   d. What magazine subscriptions do I receive to keep me up-to-date in my career?

   e. What clubs and professional organizations am I a member of?

   f. What skill proved to be the most important to my success?

   g. What jobs got me to this successful place?

   h. How do I dress?

> The things I've done in my life have required a lot of years of work before they took off.
>
> *Steven Jobs*

119

3. Don't wait until the future—use your answers like a list and go shopping for the closest match you can get to each thing you imagined right now.

That is it. That is the fastest way to achieve your dream job. For myself, this planning process shaved a good two or three years off of achieving my most recent dream job of professional speaking. In August of 1992 I decided to become a speaker on college campuses. I was starting completely from scratch, with the exception that I could speak confidently in public. I had no speech written, no business leads, no money, and no time to waste—so I started with future-perfect planning.

I closed my eyes and imagined myself far into the future at a time when I had become a very successful speaker. From this future-perfect place I saw a lot of things. I imagined that I had an office and I imagined a lot of things in my office. The first things I saw were brochures that promoted my speeches. Since I was imagining myself as super-successful, I saw the brochures as super-great—full color, high design, and covered with testimonial quotes from students all across the country. I also imagined a bookshelf with many books about public speaking, motivation, success, and college; subscriptions to magazines specifically for speakers (although I had no idea if such magazines existed); and lastly that I was a member of a speakers club. I figured that the club was where I made friends with a lot of other speakers.

After that little mental exercise, I had my shopping list and I knew that if I wanted to reach that dream as soon as

▶ **HOT TIP**

Make a business card right away for the profession you want to have. Since you don't work for a company, call yourself a consultant. For instance, a journalism student could make a card that says, "Writing Consultant." Business cards speak louder than words.

possible, I needed all that stuff as soon as possible. So I found:

- books (at the bookstore)

- magazines (at the library and through subscriptions)

- clubs/associations (advertised in the magazines)

- speaking skills (I joined my local Toastmasters so I could practice every week)

- brochures (I got them designed by a young graphic designer in exchange for a computer modem and put the printing costs on my credit card)

- mentors (asked for through the association and won with a little persistence)

Doing all these things took me about two months. Think about what I had going for me at the end of that time: I had enough tools of the trade to make speaker bureaus and college career centers take me very seriously. As a result I got a paid gig three months later, for a fee that is normally paid to speakers who have been in the business for at least three years.

Doing this future-perfect planning exercise is like hitting the fast-forward button on your success. Instead of waiting for all these things to happen to you, you make them happen as soon as possible. And the sooner you get the items on the list, the sooner things'll get cookin'.

▶ **HOT TIP**

Peruse the fantastic *Job Hunter's Sourcebook: Where to Find Employment Leads and Other Job Search Resources* by Kathleen E. Makipotts, editor. This book is incredibly thorough when it comes to listing resources you can use for your dream job—it lists professional associations, plus it tells you sources of help wanted ads, placement and job referral services, employer directories and networking lists, handbooks and manuals, employment agencies, and search firms. Look for it in your career center or library.

CHAPTER 22

Now Get Out There!

That's the Action Plan! Do the suggested activities and at graduation you'll be in a position to get a great job. What? You're not sure if you want to work after graduation???? Thinking of delaying your graduation date so that you can take a few more classes or do a few more internships? Great idea! Take as long as you like to finish school. The working world will still be there when you finish. There's really no rush, unless you're in a hurry to have more money or to reach your career dreams. Look at that course catalog and take courses just for fun (last chance before you're at work most of the time).

▶ **HOT TIP**

Just after graduation is a perfect time to do some Short-Term Job Adventures! (backdoorjobs.com)

▶ **HOT TIP**

Many grads are now marketing themselves as free agents. Employers become "clients" and jobs are "projects" as these grads move from one opportunity to the next.

Thinking of taking a year off after college to travel? Go for it!

There is no better time to travel than right after college. You're still largely free from big financial obligations like house payments, furniture bills, insurance payments, etc. And again, the working world will want you just as much when you get back. (They may even want you more because you'll have interesting stories to tell.)

Thinking of getting your master's degree? Caution!!!

There are three reasons why a lot of students start thinking about getting their master's degree near graduation, but there are only two good reason to do so. The first reason many students want to get their master's is because graduation draws near and they suddenly realize that they're not ready for the real world. They have no idea of what they want to do, no work experiences, no job leads, etc. Because they're unprepared, they've decided to get their master's degree. It sounds impressive, it delays the pressure of getting a job for another two years, and it seems like a program that will finally teach them the job skills they know they need. These students are going over Niagara Falls—a master's degree will no more prepare you for working than a bachelor's degree did. If you're panicked because you don't feel prepared, the best remedy is to get out there and work for a year. Right away you'll start building up skills and get a real sense of what work you like and don't like to do.

The second reason students want to get their master's is because so many professors recommend it. It's important to understand where your professors are coming from. A crowning jewel for professors is for one of their students to go on to get a Ph.D. and to do teaching and research. They sometimes hope students will take the higher education path because it means that they inspired you so much and taught you so well that you wanted to follow in their footsteps. And yes, if you do want to follow in one of your professor's footsteps, higher education is the required path.

The third reason many students want to get their master's is because they've heard that people with this degree get paid a lot more and have a better chance at getting a job. Some fields require an advanced degree for entry—for instance, law, medicine, scientific research, and college or university teaching. But if you're not planning to go into those fields, a master's degree will usually not increase your starting salary or give you a better chance at winning jobs, because, most of all, employers are hiring based on work experience.

▶ **HOT TIP**

The Ultimate New Employee Survival Guide by Ed Holton

▶ **HOT TIP**

Call for a FREE catalog with over 100 entrepreneurial business start-up ideas and $$ figures for each career's profit potential and average start-up investment. This catalog is an eyeopener! Entrepreneur Media Inc., (800) 421-2300, smallbizbooks.com

You can always pick up your needle and move to another groove.

Timothy Leary

So, the two good reasons for getting your master's are (1) if the career of your choice requires an advanced degree for entry; (2) if it's a dream of yours to get a master's degree. Other than those two reasons, you'd do better to just go get started on your career.

Ready to go out and get that great job?

You'll do well if you've followed the suggestions in this book because you will have the skills that employers are looking for. You are also about to job search in a world which now offers a lot more options than the traditional nine-to-five workday. For instance, you can choose from the following:

- full-time work with a big company
- full-time work with a small, growing company
- part-time work for experience and money
- volunteer work for experience
- contract work on a project basis for variety
- starting your own business

In addition to having more career options available than ever before, you are also in the midst of a job search revolution and it's crucial that you are aware and at the forefront of it. Suddenly, computers are having a major impact on the job search process. More and more each day, companies are hiring people they have found through computer databases filled with electronic resumes. Going, going, almost gone are the days when companies placed help wanted ads in the newspaper. It's more effective for them to call a resume database company and say, for instance, "Please run a computer search for a person who majored in psychology. This individual should have internship experience, be willing to relocate to Chicago, and be okay with the salary range we're offering." The resumes in the database that match the qualifications for the job will then come up on screen. So if you didn't get *your* resume into the database, you don't have a chance.

You can start taking advantage of the electronic job search revolution by posting your resume on the Internet. For instance, JobDirect Inc. (1-800-971-4884 or www. jobdirect.com) is one of many companies you can call to find out whether or not you'd like your resume placed with

▶ **HOT TIP**

These three books are filled with great advice and comprehensive lists of Internet job-finding resources:
- *Adams Electronic Job Search Almanac* by Adams (Adams Publishing)
- *Careerxroads: The 1999 Directory to Jobs, Resumes and Career Management on the World Wide Web, 4th edition,* by Mark Mehler, Gerry Crispin (Published by IEEE)
- *Electronic Resumes and Online Networking* by Rebecca Smith (Career Press)

▶ **HOT TIP**

Thought of by many to be the best gateway on the Web to job sites: *The Riley Guide,* compiled by Margaret F. Dikel (rileyguide.com).

them. (In particular JobDirect Inc. has an emphasis on entry-level jobs for students.)

Next, you can increase the range of your job search by searching the Internet's help wanted ads. A great place to begin your Internet job search is at Job Bank USA (www. jobbankusa.com/search.html).

Next, you can increase the range of your job search by using computerized job bulletin boards. Many help wanted ads are now being placed on computerized job bulletin boards which you can respond to if you know where to find them. For example, Jobtrack (1990 Westwood Blvd., Suite 260, Los Angeles, CA 90025, 1-310-474-3377) is one of many organizations you can contact that specializes in helping students access online help wanted ads.

One last thing on the electronic job search revolution: You must think of the Internet as an additional job search tool—a way to get lucky. There is a big question as to how effective the Internet is for finding employment. A lot of sources estimate that people searching for non-techy jobs have a 1 to 3 percent chance of finding their job on-line. On the other hand, people searching for technical jobs have a much better chance. Also there is another reality to getting your job via the net: Frankly, the liberal arts student with less than a 3.0 G.P.A. is S.O.L. as far as resume databases go. The traditional job search methods still count, so check out your career center or library to scoop a great book on job search strategies.

Before you start your job search there is one more bit of information that might serve you well. It's a career trend that indicates you're likely to have more jobs in your lifetime than your parents probably did. The Bureau of Labor statistics esti- mates that seven to ten jobs in a lifetime is the new norm, and that along the way you're likely to work in three com- pletely different fields. "Most new entrants in the job market can look forward to a career that progresses with all the pre- dictability of a ball ricocheting inside a pinball machine," says Howard Figler, author of *The Complete Job Search Handbook: All the Skills You Need to Get Any Job and Have a Good Time Doing It.* What does this prediction mean to you? Simply that you can be the captain of your ship, choosing and pursuing jobs you'd love, but when the winds change direction you'll have to make adjustments.

Sometimes you'll make adjustments because things don't necessarily happen when you expect them to happen. Con-

▶ **HOT TIP**

The single best site on the Web for job hunting online is Richard Bolles's *What Color Is Your Parachute: The Net Guide* (JobHuntersbible.com).

▶ **HOT TIP**

The best-selling job-hunting book in the world is Richard Nelson Bolles's *What Color Is Your Parachute?* (Ten Speed Press).

Don't just go to school. Make an impact there.

Darron Trobetsky

sider the story of Darron Trobetsky, who got his dream job at Nike two years after college. The story of how it happened is amazing.

Darron's journey to Nike began his sophomore year, when he became involved in a fraternity on campus. Little did he know that his involvement in this fraternity would later connect him to Nike. His journey continued when he did an internship at a small ad agency. Here he picked up a videotape of the Nike commercial titled "Revolution," that he would watch over and over, thinking to himself, "I would love to work at Nike."

After college he went to work for his fraternity's national office. "Every one of the ten guys I worked with knew how badly I wanted to work for Nike, so when one of them met a former Nike employee he immediately gave me his phone number." Darron wasted no time calling the man, and the man pointed him in the direction of a department called "Ekin"—an elite department of thirty people who know Nike products "front to back," hence the name *Ekin*, which is Nike spelled backwards.

Darron called the director of Ekin and things went his way immediately—the director answered the phone and happily talked for 45 minutes. The call went so well the director invited Darron to travel to Portland, Oregon for a job interview. Darron confidently accepted and went to compete with fifteen other people for five job openings. In a single day he did three different interviews that went great.

I sent thank you notes, before I left the Portland airport.

Darron Trobetsky

> *They called a week later and told me that I didn't get the job. I was super shocked and really disappointed. They told me I needed more experience in sports marketing. It was heartbreaking, but I thought to myself, "I'm going to be an Ekin someday. I just need more experience."*

He found that experience at a track cycling facility near his hometown in Trexlertown, Pennsylvania.

Nike receives over 100,000 resumes a year, even though Nike never posts a job opening.

> *I met somebody who was real important with the facility, and they needed help for the Olympic trials. I told him that I didn't care what they paid me, I was willing to volunteer. I got the job and was carrying cases of soda, writing press releases, and meeting with advertisers. Meanwhile, I kept in contact with the director at Nike, calling him to say, "Hey, here's what I'm doing—you should hire me." After a couple months he invited me back for another job interview.*

Darron's second try at Nike was in New Jersey with ten people competing for two jobs. This time Darron shined like a supernova. "I hit it out of the park! It went really great."

But Nike gave the job to two other people and told Darron, "You're on our bench." Darron remembers all his friends asking him if he got the job. "I'd answer, 'Well no, but yes. I'm up next.'"

It felt like a real setback, but still, in my heart, I didn't want to give up. To make sure I stayed on the director's mind, I'd call or send a note every two weeks. I'd clip an article from a sports trend magazine and send it along with a short note. I learned through my fraternity involvement how much people appreciate a kind note.

Then in January, four months later, something went really wrong. The director who believed in Darron so much left the company. Darron had to start over. He worked to reintroduce himself to two new people with calls and letters. After two more months it paid off. Again he was invited to interview, this time in March, and this time at Nike's headquarters in Beaverton, Oregon.

"I went into this interview with a whole new level of confidence. I didn't even take pictures of the Nike headquarters because I knew I was going to be back." Darron's first two interviews went well, but during his third and most important interview of the day, Darron noticed a bulging folder with a green card hanging out. It was sitting on the executive's desk. During the course of the interview, the executive opened the folder to retrieve something. Imagine Darron's surprise when he saw it was full of his own cards and notes. The previous director had kept everything Darron had ever sent.

Darron had been trying to get his dream job for almost a year—longer if you count the years he spent dreaming about it—and suddenly every ounce of his persistence was paying off. The third interview went great and Darron was finally hired to be an Ekin.

There is only one thing we control in life, and that's how we react. I really wanted a job at Nike and no matter how much it hurt to get turned down, I was determined to work harder and be ten times better. Even though I didn't see it, I probably wasn't ready the first two times. But now I've got a job I love more than any other job I've ever had.

> Not everyone can be born beautiful or intelligent but everyone can become effective. Yet there are very few really effective people. Any employer will employ an effective person ahead of any other person.
>
> *Edward de Bono*

▶ **HOT TIP**

Read this book—get paid top dollar. *Negotiating Your Salary: How to Make $1000 a Minute* (Ten Speed Press)

Maybe the greatest thing about Darron's story is that he knew his dream and never stopped going for it. There will be times in your life when you'll suffer setbacks but those setbacks will only be setbacks if you allow them to be. Persistence is a great habit employed by successful people, as is networking with courteous cards and phone calls. Read on, because the next section has the best stories in the whole book—stories that illustrate the six habits that will take you as far as you want to go in life.

PART 3

High Octane

The hall is rented. The orchestra is engaged.
Now it's time to dance.

Captain Picard of
Star Trek: The Next Generation

The Six Habits of Students Who Will Go Far

Success. 1. The achievement of something desired, planned, or attempted.

New College Edition of the American Heritage Dictionary

This book is building momentum and if you've been doing the suggested activities, buckle up because you're about to hit warp speed. The first two sections have covered how to get the most out of your education to prepare yourself to get a good job. The next part will show you what it takes to actually reach your dreams. (I kid you not.)

Each of the following chapters details a fundamental habit of success. If you want to make a million bucks, paint a masterpiece, solve the homelessness problem, set a world record, become a fabulous teacher, or launch your own business—the six fundamentals of success are:

1. The ability to focus on what you care about.

2. The ability to make bold decisions.

3. The desire to commit yourself to taking the time to make your dreams come true.

4. The courage to break through your failures.

5. The good sense to pay yourself 10%, first and always.

6. Being good to others.

Take these enormously powerful principles and make them into habits. When they are something you do on a consistent basis, no one can stop you from achieving your success.

CHAPTER 23

Focus—and Focus on What You Care About

Most people don't know how to begin realizing their dreams. When they try to picture the necessary steps all they see is gray. But you don't have to know all the steps to begin—all you need to know is how to get started. Starting is the most important part and you can do that by picking up a how-to book about your profession or by doing an informational interview with someone who is already in the field. After that, you really don't need a detailed plan. All you need is a focus on what you care about.

Wendy Kopp concentrated all of her energy on educational reform and produced the organization Teach for America. David Eggers focused all of his energy on publishing and produced *Might* magazine. Michael Bates focused all his energy on business and produced a software marketing corporation. Veronica Chambers directed all her energy toward writing and ended with a publishing career.

Entrepreneur, speaker, and best-selling author Anthony Robbins was called the "solutions man" in high school because he was so focused on helping people change virtually any part of their lives. He chose to develop this one ability by reading as much as he could on the subject and speaking to groups as often as possible. (Rumor has it that he skimmed more than 500 books and would often speak twice a day to anyone who would listen.) This singular focus and relentless pursuit paid off BIG. At just 32, Anthony had two number one national bestsellers, *Unlimited Power* (Fawcett Book Group, 1987) and *Awaken the Giant Within* (Simon and Schuster, 1992); and when he came to speak in San Francisco, thousands of people came out and lined up hours

If you want to win anything—a race, your self, your life—you have to go a little berserk.

George Sheehan, physician and author

It's not what we do once in a while that shapes our lives. It's what we do consistently.

Anthony Robbins, best-selling author of Awaken the Giant Within *(Simon & Schuster)*

early. (Public speakers don't usually get that kind of rock star treatment.)

One of my most influential mentors is Leland Russell, a man who can (practically) leap tall buildings in a single bound. Leland graced the pages of *Life* magazine as a rock band member, was the stage manager for Billy Joel and many other famous acts, the founder and CEO of a national real estate company, and now creates highly acclaimed multimedia leadership programs. Leland once greatly contributed to my success by telling me, "Patrick, you scatter your energy on too many things at once. Results are produced by focus. If you focus light on a single point, you get a laser beam. When you concentrate all your energy on what you care about the most, you'll get outstanding results."

I took his advice and chose to focus all my energy on becoming a great public speaker because every time I've seen one I've thought to myself, "That's what I'd love to do." When I made speaking my focus and relegated my other interests to hobbies, I suddenly started to get outstanding results. It seemed like everything that began to happen in my life revealed a piece of new information about my career: Something on TV would spark an idea; helpful articles started showing up in the newspaper; ideas started coming to me in the middle of the night; books were suddenly available on my subject; and inexplicably, I started bumping into people who could help me advance my career. I began to feel like I was being guided toward my dreams.

What was happening to me was the "Volkswagen Bug" phenomenon: If you begin to look for a Volkswagen Bug to buy, you'll suddenly start seeing them everywhere! Remember, your mind is like a bloodhound. If you give it a single scent, it will dig up every clue in its path until it reaches its target. But if you don't give it a strong lead to follow, it will pick up a lot of false trails.

A speaker named Kevin Hughes recently reminded me of something very important. He pointed out just how incredibly unique each one of us is. Using scientific probability estimates, he proved that the probability of a person just like you being born is less than the chances of a chunk of gold spontaneously forming in a glass of water! In other words, you are a possibility that has never occurred before and will never occur again.

If you want a quality, act as if you already had it. Try the "as if" technique.

William James, psychologist

I've always been able to write and draw, BUT there's a million people who have the same skills. Skills are such a small percentage of what it takes.

David Eggers

The happiest people spend much time in a state of flow—the state in which people are so involved in an activity that nothing else seems to matter; the experience itself is so enjoyable that people will do it even at great cost, for the sheer sake of doing it.

Mihaly Csikszentmihalyi

▶ **HOT TIP**
Read *Do It! Let's Get off Our Buts* by John-Roger and Peter McWilliams (Prelude Press).

No one else has had or will ever have your unique combination of talents, experiences, and dreams. So don't waste that uniqueness. Maybe you've got the combination it takes to find a cure for AIDS or the composition for the next Mona Lisa. Or maybe you've got what it takes to do equally great things of lower profile or less apparent significance. Maybe you can teach students in a way that will change their lives or speak to groups of people and motivate them to do things they never thought they could. Whatever you choose to do, you'll achieve it once you focus on what you care about.

Remember, the person who ends up doing the best is rarely the person who was the most gifted to begin with. The one on top is usually the one who prepared, practiced, and was willing to make sacrifices to achieve their success—in other words, the one who was focused. No matter who you are or what you have or haven't done, you have this guarantee: Once you focus on what you care about, you will become talented. Talent isn't necessarily a gift, it is a product of being focused.

All of the people I interviewed for this book admit to the difficulty of learning their primary talent. Yet all of them achieved their goals because they were focused on what they cared about.

Most people diffuse their psychic energy (attention) in hundreds of random ways. Those who flow focus their psychic energy intentionally upon the task at hand. It really boils down to knowing your goal, concentrating upon it, remaining determined, and having the self-discipline to complete what you are doing.
Dick Sutphen, writer and spiritualist

CHAPTER 24

Make Bold Decisions

Everything about the schooling process encourages you to act rationally and think slowly and carefully about all your "big" decisions. Granted, many decisions in life—like choosing a school or buying a home—require this kind of slow decision-making process. But there are moments in life that require big decisions immediately and without rational analysis.

For instance, if you're in a desperate situation, you have to be able to do something fast before the situation becomes a crisis. If you're feeling inspired to do something courageous, you've only got a short time before the inspiration will give way to fear. If the window of opportunity presents itself, that window will not stay open for very long unless you climb through. In each of the following stories, I guarantee you that if the person had thought long and hard about doing what they felt inspired to do, they would have talked themselves out of a good thing. You can't be perfectly rational about everything.

For 24-year-old Wendy Kopp, hers was a bold decision to create a national teaching organization. She remembers telling her Princeton thesis advisor that she was going to get the $2.5 million needed to launch the project from Texas billionaire Ross Perot. "After all, I'm from Dallas, he's from Dallas. I'll just write him a letter." Not a particularly rational maneuver, but she boldly did just that. He didn't reply the first time she wrote, but one day "the phone rang in my office, and the secretary said the call was from Ross Perot. I thought at first she was kidding. But when I heard that Texas drawl on the line, I knew it was true." Ross Perot gave her $500,000.

Seventeen-year-old Bill Gates made a bold and irrational decision to pick up the telephone, call the man who was

You are just one bold decision away.

Do you realize if we were playing by the rules we'd be in gym?
Dialog from the movie
Ferris Bueller's Day Off

134

making the first personal computer, and announce that he had written a computer program called BASIC—which he hadn't actually written yet. Bill programmed for eight solid weeks to back up the claim he'd made over the phone. The results of this bold move? You know the rest. He is estimated to become the world's first trillionaire.

For college senior Nancy Collins, interviewing a celebrity for her Reporting 101 class (instead of the assigned interview from "your aunt, boyfriend, or roommate") was a bold decision. She didn't have any connections to celebrities, but she did know that performer Rod McKuen was selling out shows in the town she lived in. How her bold decision played itself out is quite a story:

> With my boyfriend Tom, I proceeded to the concert and, the minute McKuen moaned his last lyric, rushed to the stage door, where I blithely announced to the guard that I was from the Boston Globe, there to interview Mr. McKuen. The guard left and returned with McKuen's manager, who looked puzzled but interested. Five minutes later, I'd sold him on my nonexistent credentials, and we were being ushered into the singer's dressing room, which was packed with people. Immediately, the crowd clammed up—my first inkling of the undeserved awe the press engendered. But now what? Tommy's elbow digging into my left side flicked my mental switch, and I started asking questions, frantically scribbling McKuen's every utterance in a stenographer's notebook. With each question (three into it, and I still hadn't been found out!), my courage grew and my curiosity took over. What a ride! Internally wired, externally calm, I Zenned out as the world around me fell away. It was just me and McKuen, who, at that moment, might as well have been Walt Whitman. Thirty minutes later, I sailed out of that room, hooked. I had found It. The thing I loved doing more than anything else in the world, the thing that came most naturally: getting people to talk about their lives.

A few weeks later, Nancy's McKuen interview was run in a small Boston paper. In her own words:

> Upon seeing my byline, my second thoughts about foregoing acting were quickly dispelled. "My God, what a wonderful

Life is either a daring adventure or nothing.

Helen Keller,
deaf and blind lecturer

There's moments in your life that make you, that set the course for who you're going to be.
"Angel" on Buffy, The Vampire Slayer

I would go into a place and say, "I'm a comedian," and they'd say, "Get out of here." Then I'd put a fifty-dollar bill on the bar. I'd say, "Just let me tell some jokes, and if people leave or I embarrass the customers, you keep the fifty." The wager always worked.

Jay Leno

Do not be too timid and squeamish about your actions. All life is an experiment.
Ralph Waldo Emerson, essayist and poet

Be bold and mighty forces will come to your aid.
Basil King, writer

Don't play for safety—it's the most dangerous thing in the world.
Hugh Walpole, writer

business," I thought. "And you don't even have to have a license." Clearly, this was a great job for a maverick. All I needed was my mind and a notebook. It was my ticket to adventure, my passport to power, my visa to the most important thinkers in the world.

Today Nancy Collins is at the top of her field and she's interviewed the biggest celebrities in the business.

One of my bold and irrational but successful decisions was to write this book. I was inspired by a newspaper article about a student who had written a book and instantly I decided to write a competing one. If I had thought more about the endeavor, I know I would have talked myself out of it. At the time I was in a different job, I didn't know exactly what I would write about, I had never written much, and I didn't have any contacts in the publishing business. But I made the decision to just do it and a year and a half later I had a publishing deal.

Many of the biggest, most exciting things in your life will happen because you made a bold and irrational decision. Granted, it's the actions we take after making a decision that actually produce results, but it's the decisions to take action that set everything in motion in the first place.

The decisions we make every day shape our future . . . and so do the decisions we don't make. A lot of the decisions we shy away from are the ones that we don't know how we'd pull off. I only need to tell you this: Bill Gates didn't know how he'd get the software done on time or if it would actually work; Wendy Kopp didn't know how she'd raise millions of dollars; Nancy Collins didn't know how she'd get a celebrity interview or what questions she'd ask; and I didn't know how I'd pull off this book. Bold decisions are bold precisely because of the uncertainty involved.

Life is simply too short not to take risks. I worked with a college student one summer who had gotten his dream job—playing video games—because he made the decision to cold call a company on the other side of the country and ask for his dream job. The bolder the decision, the higher the pay-off. I think the boldest decision a person can make is to live life in an extraordinary way. Decide that no matter what you do with your life, you won't settle for "average," "pretty good," or "OK." Make a bold decision for yourself right now.

CHAPTER 25

Commit Yourself to Taking the Time to Make Your Dreams Come True

As Win Borden said, "There is a big difference between impatience and the results it produces, and persistence and the results you can achieve." If you really want to be successful, a long-term outlook is a necessary factor. When you plan your goals, don't just think about what you could accomplish in three months or a year—think about what you could accomplish in five to ten years. When you make a long-term commitment, the possibilities change dramatically.

Veronica Chambers got the amazing opportunity to cowrite a book with movie director John Singleton because for two years she mailed him something every two weeks. Whether it was a sample of her writing or an update on her career, she never asked him for anything, just let him know who she was and what she was up to. After two years of this mail campaign, the phone rang one day and it was John Singleton calling to offer her a job. That's what a long-term effort can do for a person!

In *The Man Who Planted Trees* (Chelsea House, 1987), Jean Giorno describes a man who lived by himself in the middle of a barren, sandy land. Every day the man would tend to his sheep and plant a handful of tree seeds. Day after day, month after month, and year after year he did this—for over 30 years.

Do you know what happens when you plant a few tree seeds every day for over 30 years? You get a small forest and that small forest begins to grow and multiply on its own. Next, a forest changes the climate patterns in the area. Rainfall increases and puts rivers where there were none. Animals move into the new home and life starts to flourish.

You've just got to keep in mind that Stove Top stuffing did not replace potatoes in a day.

Ellen Degeneres

People usually overestimate what they can accomplish in a year and dramatically underestimate what they can accomplish in a decade.

Anthony Robbins

My original vision of a personal computer on every desk and every home will take more than 15 more years to achieve so there will be more than 30 years since I first got excited about that goal. My work is not like sports where you actually win a game and it's over after a short period of time.

Bill Gates

137

Rain puts a hole in stone because of its constancy, not its force. I just kept knocking on doors until the right one opened.

H. Joseph Gerber, entrepreneur

When we watch a great musician or top athlete in action, we see a performance that may take only a few minutes. What we don't see is the hours of perspiration and preparation that enabled him or her to become great. The Michael Jordans and the Chris Everetts of the world have talent, yes, but they're also the first ones on and the last ones off the basketball or tennis court.

Harvey B. Mackay

Success isn't something you chase. It's something you have to put forth the effort for constantly. Then maybe it'll come when you least expect it.

Michael Jordan

You bust your butt hitting balls, practicing chipping and putting, working on your game. And lo and behold you hit that magical shot.

Tiger Woods

And finally, a community of people move in because the land is again hospitable. One man planting a few tree seeds every day for 30 years can produce those results!

The amount of time you're willing to commit to reaching a dream is directly related to the probability of your making the dream a reality. Being talented or successful at something is nearly impossible if you're not willing to dedicate a sufficient amount of time to developing your skills. But if you're willing to dedicate yourself to the time it takes, you've practically got a guarantee that you will succeed.

Let's say you decide that you want to become a guitar player. If you say you're going to give it a go for a year, you're probably not going to be the next Keith Richards. But if you say that you're going to commit to it for ten years, I bet you'll at least end up on a CD. As a matter of fact, you'd probably be good after only five years, but the second five years would move you into the "excellent" category.

Many years of daily effort creates pure excellence. Somebody once said to a master pianist, "I'd give half of my life if I could play piano like you." And she replied, "Good, because that's about how long it takes." Arthur Rubenstein, the great pianist, once said, "If I miss one day of practice, I notice the difference. If I miss two days of practice, the critics notice the difference. If I miss three days of practice, the audience notices the difference."

Almost nobody wants to work on something every day. But some people do it anyway. Greg LeMond, three-time winner of the Tour de France cycling race, explained why he does it: "There are many times I wish I was playing 18 holes of golf instead of training in miserable cold weather. But in the final analysis, I'd rather win the Tour de France than play 18 holes of golf. That's why I do it."

There's a mental trick that can help you see daily work as progress instead of as a chore. It's a trick based on the premise that people at the bottom of an organization think in terms of three months to a year, while people at the top think in terms of ten to 50 years. Here's the trick: Make many of your decisions according to their outcome ten years from now. If you wanted to learn to play the guitar, you might say to yourself, "Sure, for the next two or three years I'll suck, but ten years from now I'm sure to be great—and that'll leave me with plenty of years to enjoy my talent." A similar thought motivated me to launch myself as a public speaker when I was 26. I figured I'd be a great public speaker, at the latest, by 36 years old and I've met enough people over 80 to know that 36 is still young.

There are very few cases of overnight success. Most success cases—including rock bands who seem to explode out of nowhere—involve longer term persistence and commitment to an interest. Consider Conan O'Brien's commitment. "In the '80s I was doing improv in a basement and I told myself, 'This will lead to good things!' If I'd been realistic, I'd have said, 'Give up the performing thing. You're almost thirty. It's not going to happen.'" Commit yourself to reaching your goals, put in daily effort, and time will fly and your talents will soar. And . . .

Take Time

Take time to work.
It is the price of success.

Take time to think.
It is the source of power.

Take time to play.
It is the secret of perpetual youth.

Take time to read.
It is the foundation of wisdom.

Take time to be friendly.
It is the road to happiness.

Take time to dream.
It is hitching your wagon to a star.

Take time to love and be loved.
It is the privilege of the gods.

Take time to look around.
The day is too short to be selfish.

Take time to laugh.
It is the music of the soul.

Author unknown

P.S. Notice that the word "try" is absent from this chapter. The word "try" isn't in the chapter because it's a chapter about committing to do something—and "committing" to do something is almost the opposite of "trying" to do something. As Yoda said in *The Empire Strikes Back*, "Do or do not. There is no try."

Success Takes Time
- David Letterman worked for 13 years in television to get his *Late Show*.
- Jay Leno worked for six years before he did his first *Tonight Show* appearance.
- Daryl Hannah did nine movies before her first hit movie, *Splash*.
- It took Arnold Schwarzenegger five years to win the Mr. Universe bodybuilding championship.

The key to Schwarzenegger's success has always been hard work. He pumped iron harder than anyone else, and then he threw himself into a movie career with such energy and determination that he became, against all the odds and despite his Austrian accent, the no. 1 movie star in the world.

Roger Ebert, movie critic

It's said that good things come to those who wait. I believe that good things come to those who work.

Wilt Chamberlain, basketball star

It's important to be a self-starter. Nobody is going to wind you up in the morning and give you a pep talk and push you out. You have to have a firm faith and belief in yourself.

Lou Holtz, football coach at University of Notre Dame

CHAPTER 26

Break Through Your Failures

Success is the ability to go from one failure
to another with no loss of enthusiasm.

Winston Churchill

A person's ability to grow and succeed is largely related to their ability to suffer embarrassment.
Doug Engelbart,
"father of personal computers"

What I think of as "breakthroughs," R. Buckminster Fuller called "Great Moments." What we're both referring to are those embarrassing moments when what you try to do goes painfully wrong. Like the time Oprah Winfrey was dumped as an anchorwoman. Or the time David Letterman's first TV show got canceled due to poor ratings. Or the time Johnny Carson told Jay Leno he wasn't ready for an appearance on the *Tonight Show*.

There's really only one remedy for mistakes, failures, and rejections: You've got to get through them. After all, success has nothing to do with not making mistakes. Remember, when you were learning to walk, you probably fell a hundred times, but it never occurred to you that you "just weren't meant to walk." Making a mistake is just like falling down: It hurts and it feels like a good reason to stop. But the people who succeed are consistently the ones who get back up and keep going.

A professional writer is an amateur who didn't quit.
Richard Bach

I've seen a lot of people who interpret their mistakes or failures as a sure sign that it's quitting time. But I've also seen people who see their mistakes and failures as stepping stones to the next level.

Consider what happened to Dan O'Brien. Dan was the probable favorite for winning the 1992 Olympic Decathlon event. Because a gold medal was so likely for Dan, he was being featured in commercials which were calling him the world's greatest athlete. But despite the attention, when the Olympic Trials rolled around Dan did so poorly (on world-

140

wide television) that he didn't even make the Olympic Team. Talk about failure!! Many people worried that because of such an enormous public embarrassment Dan would quit the sport. But instead of letting the failure stop him, he opted to work out harder than before, and two months later he broke the world record. That's breaking through your mistakes.

Dan O'Brien is an example of how failures and mistakes happen even after you've become a winner. But Step One is getting through the many mistakes that happen when you're just starting out. Katie Couric, the cohost of the NBC *Today Show*, had an enormously painful setback at the beginning of her TV career. Her first big break came soon after college when CNN offered her a chance to cover White House news. She remembers "putting on my little blazer, combing my hair, getting to the White House, and I'm ready to go on, I have my ear piece in, and during a commercial I hear one Atlanta anchor saying to another, 'Who is that girl? She looks 16 years old.' I was crushed." She also had a voice that wasn't ready for prime-time television. It was too piercing and her southern accent was too strong. Needless to say, her first television appearance was her last for a while. "I still have that tape at home. I was a disaster," she recalls. But she didn't give up. She overcame her weaknesses by working with a speech coach. After about three years her lessons paid off and she became a prize-winning television reporter in Miami.

Suffering the embarrassment of mistakes is a little easier when you remember this: The embarrassment of a mistake or failure passes quickly; the advances you'll make last a lifetime. R. Buckminster Fuller pointed out that every advance the human race has ever made—everything we've learned—is the result of billions and billions of mistakes. So when you see a person who's able to do something really well, remember that you are looking at a person who's made it through hundreds and hundreds of mistakes.

Jon Stewart, host of *The Daily Show*, has a story to tell about his initial failure. "My first gig was pretty miserable. I wrote five minutes of material, went up there, lasted three minutes, and got heckled. And my comeback was like, 'Shut up. I'm not an asshole. You're an asshole.' I was pretty crushed because I sucked. But to some extent, it was seductive, because there was a laugh or two."

Acts:
- On their way to the moon, rockets are off course 80% of the time.
- It took over 16,000 practice launches before rockets were ready to carry humans.
- Babe Ruth struck out 1,300 times. On average he struck out once every game.
- *Chicken Soup for the Soul* was rejected by 36 publishers.

FAILURE
Failure taught me that failure isn't the end unless you give up.
Jim Carrey

I don't want to fail, but I'm not afraid to.
Michael Jordan

If at first you don't succeed, think how many people you've made happy.
H. Duane Black

Morpheus: Everyone falls the first time. If you never know failure, how can you know success?
From the movie The Matrix

My own personal mistakes are many and have sometimes been painful. Once during college when I was trying to write a good cover letter, my mentor essentially told me (in kind words) that my first draft was horrible. That hurt! But it hurt even more when she said my second and third drafts weren't very good either.

Now, if you had already put in over 15 hours of writing and you'd again been told that your writing was bad, what would you do? (A) Tell your mentor that she wouldn't know a masterpiece if it hit her in the face. (B) Break down crying and beg her not to tell anyone that you are such a bad writer. (C) Suffer the embarrassment again in hopes of getting it right. If you were stubborn and answered C, then you'd probably get the same results I did. She called my fourth draft "great" and told me I could be a talented writer. From that experience I learned that before you can walk you have to crawl.

When things seem to be going wrong, you can also think about this story which has been attributed to both ancient China and India. A villager went to the local wise man for help because his horse had run away and it was time for harvesting. In response to the villager's distress, the wise man said, "Who can tell if it's good or bad?" The disgruntled villager went home only to find that his horse had returned, bringing a mare with him. Now the man had two horses to help him with the harvesting. "Who can tell if it's good or bad?" said the wise man. The villager left but came back the next day because his son, his only helper, broke his leg while trying to work with the new mare. What was the farmer to do without a helper? "Who can tell if it's good or bad?" said the wise man. The villager was beginning to lose respect for the wise man so he left. But he came back once again the very next day, happy. The king's soldiers had swept through the area, drafting every able-bodied lad for battle, but because the farmer's son had a broken leg, he was spared. "Who can tell if it's good or bad?"

Remember, you are only human and cannot be expected to know all of the answers all of the time. However, remembering the rules on the following page might get you through some tough times.

The Rules For Being Human

(author unknown)

1. **You will receive a body.** You may like it or hate it, but it will be yours for the entire period this time around.

2. **You will learn lessons.** You are enrolled in a full-time, informal school called life. Each day in this school you will have the opportunity to learn lessons. You may like the lessons or think them irrelevant and stupid.

3. **There are no mistakes, only lessons.** Growth is a process of trial and error, experimentation. The "failed" experiments are as much a part of the process as the experiment that ultimately "works."

4. **A lesson is repeated until it is learned.** A lesson will be presented to you in various forms until you have learned it. When you have learned it you can go on to the next lesson.

5. **Learning lessons does not end.** There is no part of life that does not contain its lessons. If you are alive, there are lessons to be learned.

6. **"There" is no better than "here."** When your "there" has become a "here," you will simply obtain another "there" that will, again, look better than "here."

7. **Others are merely mirrors of you.** You cannot love or hate something about another person unless it reflects to you something you love or hate about yourself.

8. **What you make of your life is up to you.** You have all the tools and resources you need; what you do with them is up to you. The choice is yours.

9. **The answers lie inside you.** The answers to life's questions lie inside you. All you need to do is look, listen, and trust.

10. **YOU WILL FORGET ALL THIS.**

I've got to keep breathing. It'll be my worst business mistake if I don't.

> Sir Nathan Meyer Rothschild,
> first earl of Rothschild

Fall seven times, stand up eight.

> Japanese proverb

Many of life's failures are people who did not realize how close they were to success when they gave up.

> Thomas Edison

You don't learn, evolve, become more of a human being by winning Oscars, making money, and living in Malibu. You learn by disappointments.

> Jodie Foster, actress

Never give in. Never. Never. Never. Never.

> Winston Churchill

CHAPTER 27

Pay Yourself 10%
First and Always

Four years after graduating, while I was running around my neighborhood track, I met Frank Batmale, a 53-year-old fireman. We got to talking and Frank said to me, "A guy at your age could be very wealthy by my age if you started saving a little money every year." He went on to say, "I've been saving a lot of money since my early forties, but with investing, time is more important than the amount of money you put away. If I had known to start at your age, I'd be a rich, rich man."

I wanted to know more, so Frank kindly gave me a book called *The Richest Man in Babylon* by George S. Clason (New American Library). The first chapter of this tiny, best-selling book changed my life. It made me realize that since the day I started working—even during college—I've had a river of gold flowing through my hands but never kept any for myself. That river was made up of my paychecks. So I began writing my savings account a check for 10% of what I earned, before I did anything else with the money. Pay myself first— I liked that idea! After all, I was the one who earned the money, did the work, and put in the hours. And it seemed like a surefire way to build up a big savings, much better than paying all my bills first and hoping I had some left over (because I never had "leftover money"). The strange part was that it didn't seem like I had any less money to spend. The great part is that 10% of every paycheck I earn is now mine for keeps.

Before you do anything with your take-home pay, write yourself a check first. Think about the total amount of money you've earned in your lifetime and then think about how much you've kept for yourself. There are a lot of great reasons to sock 10% away. First of all, it ends up as money that benefits you 100%. It doesn't go to bill collectors—it goes only to you. Second, because it will be money that you completely control, you can invest in anything you want. Nobody will be able to tell you what you have to do with that money. Third, because of the financial freedom it earns you, if you consistently save 10% of your earnings eventually you'll have so much money that you won't have to depend on anyone else for a paycheck!

How will the meager 10% you save make you rich? A giant fortune begins with only a little money (as long you invest it in something that's earning interest). Check this scenario out:

Let's say you start saving when you're 20 and save $2,000 per year for five years. If you quit saving when you're 25 and let the money earn 12% interest in a tax-deferred investment until you're 64, through the power of compounding interest your savings will grow to over $1 million! That's over a 1,000% return on your investment!! Even if you don't intend to keep the savings for that long, the money you save goes to work creating more money!

Before you jump to the conclusion that it would be impossible to save $2,000 per year for five years, consider this: All you have to earn to save $2,000 a year is $20,000 a year. I know 99% of those in college don't earn anywhere near that much, but when you graduate you probably will. And start the minute you read this, because time is the all-important factor in obtaining wealth through the power of compounding interest.

If you delay and don't start until you're 35, there's almost no way you can catch up—even if you save $2,000 every year from 35 to 64 years old, you'll only end up with less than $500,000. The earlier you start saving, the more you'll make. And if the payback times I'm mentioning seem like forever, maybe this example will help:

If, when you were one year old, you had sold all your baby belongings and put $1,000 into savings, you'd have $6,130 by the time you were 16, $10,803 on your twenty-first birthday, $19,040 at 26, and $59,000 at 36 years old. And $1.5 million by the time you hit 64! And that's just with one payment! Thirty-five years seems like it will never arrive, but all of a sudden, there you are.

When you get there, there is no there there. But there will be a pool.

David Zucker

I found the road to wealth when I decided that a part of all I earn was mine to keep.

George S. Clason

It's easy to think that there are many months when you can't afford to pay yourself 10%. But ask yourself this: How often do you call your boss and say, "This has been a particularly tough month and I can't afford to pay my social security tax, my FICA tax, and my state tax—please don't deduct them this month." You could say that to your boss but he'd treat you like you were crazy. Taxes have to be paid no matter what. That's why Dr. David Schwartz, author of *The Magic of Thinking Success* (Wilshire Book Co., 1987), suggests you call your 10% self-payment a Financial Freedom Tax. He says, "To reap the benefits of your hard work and pull yourself out of economic slavery, you must pay your FFT just as you pay the other taxes. Remember, the FFT is the only tax you'll ever pay that goes to work for you and those you love. All other taxes are paid to people you don't know for purposes you may or may not approve of."

One other thing—paying yourself 10 percent first will be a heck of a lot easier if you don't buy items that lose value over time—like new cars. Did you know the moment you drive a new car off the lot it loses a huge chunk of its value? Yes-siree! On average, new automobiles lose more than 20 percent of their value in just their first year. Not buying something expensive that's going to lose one-fifth of its value can make a huge difference in your bank roll. For example, imagine that you have $20,000 of extra money after one year of working full-time and you decide you need to buy a car. Instead of spending $15,000 on a new car, and losing $3,000 of value in the first year, let's say you decide to shop around for a cool used convertible—and get one for $8,000. Your first big benefit is that your convertible will probably be worth $7,000 by the year's end, figuring you don't smash up the tail fins. Your further good fortune is that you still have $12,000 to invest instead of the $5,000 you'd have had you bought new. (Let's not forget car insurance and registration is a lot more expensive for new cars.) Let that $12,000 grow at an average of 15 percent per year and you'll have over $48,500 in ten years. Not bad at all—especially compared to the many new car buyers you'll know who still don't get more dates and who have a whole heck of a lot less money in the bank. Leave that money in the bank for another ten years and it becomes about $200,000! P.S.—Did I mention that Sam Walton, founder of Walmart, drove a used pick-up till the day he died? Maybe that's what made him so rich.

If you don't look ahead, nobody will—there's no time to kill.

Clint Black, singer

Studies have estimated that for every 100 people in the U.S., at retirement age 36 will be dead, 36 will be broke, 5 will still be working, 4 will be retired, and 1 will have financial freedom.

CHAPTER 28

Be Good to Others

At this point in the book, you've read about several funda-mentals of success: the ability to focus on what you care about; the ability to make bold decisions; the desire to com-mit yourself to taking the time to make your dreams come true; the courage to break through your failures; the good sense to pay yourself 10%, first and always. Nonetheless, you can put focus, commitment, boldness, persistence, and even money to work for you and not end up successful if you don't make people around you feel good about themselves.

Numerous writers have told the story of an ancient but nearly forgotten Christian monastery. No new monks had joined in years, and one by one the elderly ones were dying off. Eventually only five aged monks were left, and the monastic order seemed near extinction. Then one day, while one of the monks was walking in the nearby forest, he en-countered an equally aged wise-looking rabbi. He explained the situation to the rabbi and asked him if he had any advice. The rabbi replied with great seriousness and certainty, "I can't give you any advice, but I can tell you this: One of you five monks is the Messiah."

Stunned, the monk returned to his monastery and passed this news on to the others. At first everyone was shocked, but slowly they became more and more accustomed to the idea, and eventually, whenever they would encounter one another, each would think, "Perhaps he's the Messiah." But there wasn't any way to actually determine which one of them was the Messiah, and none of them really felt that he was the one. So they all began to act as if any of them might be the Messiah—treating each other with great love, compassion, and respect. As a result, things began to change. People who passed through were impressed by the love and respect that radiated from each of the monks. Word about the monastery

Great people create great acts of kindness.

Cervantes

May I never get too busy in my own affairs that I fail to respond to the needs of others with kindness and compassion.

Thomas Jefferson

We are here on earth to do good to others. What the others are here for, I don't know.

W. H. Auden, poet and essayist

Many of the things you can count don't count. Many of the things you can't count, really count.

Albert Einstein, physicist

147

spread, and younger men came to investigate. Soon the monastery was thriving again and the tradition continued with renewed spirit and energy.

In many ways, we're all pretty much the same when it comes to our aspirations. We all want to feel likable, important, and good about the things we do. Nothing feels better than meeting someone who recognizes our importance, accomplishments, and good qualities. Think about the people you would do anything for—aren't they people that like, praise, or admire you? A brief piece by an anonymous author may help you keep in mind the impact other people have had in your life, and the impact you can have on theirs.

Do you remember who gave you your first break?

Someone saw something in you once. That's partly why you are where you are today. It could have been a thoughtful parent, a perceptive teacher, a demanding drill sergeant, an appreciative employer, or just a friend who dug down in his pocket and came up with a few bucks. Whoever it was had the kindness and the foresight to bet on your future. These are two beautiful qualities that separate the human being from the orangutan. In the next 24 hours, take ten minutes to write a grateful note to the person who helped you. You'll keep a wonderful friendship alive. Matter of fact, take another ten minutes to give somebody else a break. Who knows? Someday you might get a nice letter. It could be one of the most gratifying messages you ever read.

If you want help while you move toward your goals, help the people around you move toward theirs first. If you want compliments for the things you accomplish or the traits you possess, first give the people around you compliments that they deserve. If you want people to notice your gifts, first notice theirs. If you want to benefit from other people's expertise, give other people the benefit of yours. The point is people will treat you as well as you treat them.

One summer, I worked with a college student named Randy, who was actively pursuing his dream job. At only 20 he was already focused on what he cared about, committed to putting in lots of extra effort, overcoming mistakes, and even making bold decisions. But when it came to helping the other college students we were working with, Randy was unavailable. He kept everything he knew to himself in hopes of having a competitive advantage. The most shocking instance was when he flatly refused to tell another student

> What you remember, what you measure yourself by, what you cling to as you get older is what you have done as a family, what you have done for others, your own naked humanity.
>
> *Barbara Bush, former first lady*

> No one will ever love you for your work or accomplishments. People will love you for the way you make them feel.
>
> *Something my mom taught me*

▶ **HOT TIP**

There's a good on-line article about being good to others through networking: franklinquest.com/priorities/ vol2issue3_career.html how to get a VIP to go to lunch with you—something Randy knew very well how to do. He paid a high price to keep what he felt were his "competitive secrets." By the end of the summer, all the other team members, including myself, had isolated him, and he confided in me that the situation caused him great stress and disappointment. What goes around, comes around.

Too many people believe that if you give away good advice, you give away your secret recipe. And that if you give someone a great compliment, you suddenly become a lesser person. Both assumptions are false! You could give away all the good advice you have and still not have given away your competitive edge because your competitive edge is you— your unique blend of personality, talent, and experience. You could give the highest compliments in the world without ever implying that you are any less.

Are you in the habit of giving compliments? There's a lot of ways to get started. Compliment people about their appearance, about their ideas, accomplishments, family, or interests; about their material possessions, their name, the way they answer a phone; about their smile, the way they speak; how well they listen; or even about how nicely they compliment you! Compliment people on anything you genuinely like. (The key is being genuine.) No matter how far you go, or how much you excel, never forget that each person you meet does something that is worthy of your admiration. Treat everyone with the same respect and attention that you hope they'll give you and you will greatly increase your chances of being greeted by smiles and helping hands.

When I was growing up, my mother would often say, "Always take time to make people around you feel good about themselves—your attention can change a person's life and it leaves you feeling wonderful." I discovered you really can change a person's life the day someone changed mine. One of my college roommates told me I had a gift for sharing my enthusiasm with others. That single, positive comment gave me a deep-seated belief that I could someday use this gift to help others.

My story pales in comparison to the true life story of Carl Lewis, the most successful track and field star in history, who won nine Olympic gold medals. As a kid his destiny was deeply impacted by three simple words. When Carl was a kid, his parents took him to meet track legend Jesse Owens. "He said three things, and I took it as encouragement, and it lasted for a long time. Can you believe it? He said three or four words, and look what an effect it had on me. Owens didn't even

> If you help others, you will be helped, perhaps tomorrow, perhaps in one hundred years, but you will be helped. Nature must pay off the debt … It is a mathematical law and all life is mathematics.
>
> *G. I. Gurdjieff, philosopher*

> Too often we underestimate the power of a touch, a smile, a kind word, a listening ear, or the smallest act of caring, all of which have the potential to turn a life around.
>
> *Leo Buscaglia*

> You have not lived a perfect day, unless you've done something for someone who will never be able to repay you.
>
> *Ruth Smeltzer*

know me personally. He was encouraging a little kid. He said, 'You could be good,' and I believed it. I totally did."

A friend of mine, Christian Haren, has used his gifts to help others, and in doing so has expanded my understanding about the power of treating people well. Christian has led an almost mythical existence. In his lifetime, he's been a marine, a top male model, an actor both on screen and stage, he's written a screenplay, owned and lived on a ranch, and attended some top-notch universities. He is also one of the longest surviving people afflicted with AIDS.

After being diagnosed with AIDS eight years ago, Christian was told that he only had a short time to live. However, he has not only survived, but for the past seven years he's been reaching out to thousands of youths, parents, and educators all across the country as a teacher of AIDS awareness. Almost daily, Christian is giving love, joy, and hope to people he's never met, and he gets an abundance back in return. After years of loneliness, despite his fortune and fame, he says, "Finally I'm in the process of joining the human race." What has kept him going? Christian has a guess: "I think all the love and joy I've gotten from people over the past eight years has kept me alive for so long."

There is no scarcity when it comes to smart advice, genuine compliments, or good, old-fashioned loving actions—so use all of them to make other people feel better about themselves. Nothing will make you feel better on the inside, and nothing will bring you more true love and affection. Honestly, who doesn't like love and affection?!

Let me end this chapter with a brief piece by Ralph Waldo Emerson.

Success

To laugh often and much;
To win the respect of intelligent people
and the affection of children;
To earn the appreciation of honest critics
and endure the betrayal of false friends;
To appreciate beauty;
To find the best in others;
To leave the world a bit better, whether by a healthy child, a
garden patch or a redeemed social condition;
To know even one life has breathed easier because you
have lived;
This is to have succeeded.

CHAPTER 29

Bon Voyage!

There is no better time than right after
graduation to be terribly idealistic,
uncompromising, and gutsy. My advice is simple:
Go for it. Life is not a game to be won; it is a
game to be played. To the players go the game.

Donald Asher

You've now considered your interests, passions, and aspirations. You've brainstormed future job possibilities that match who you truly are. You've begun to disarm some of your fears. You've started doing the activities that make you very valuable in the working world. And you've learned the habits that create success. Now treat yourself to a few thoughts about what is possible for you.

- It's possible for you to end up in the career of your dreams.

- It's possible for you to live a life that is rich with enthusiasm and fulfillment.

- It's possible for you to accomplish so much that magazines like *Life* want to write articles about you.

When someone knows what they want out of life, knows that there are many ways to turn their passions into a career, and when someone is motivated by dreams—they truly have most of what it takes to turn their dreams into reality.

Maybe you're smart, maybe you're not—who cares?! Maybe you came from a wealthy and supportive background, maybe you didn't—who cares?! Maybe you're motivated by a lot of things, maybe by a few. It doesn't matter. What matters is focusing on what really motivates you most and giving your dreams a chance. Still not convinced that it's possible to allow your dreams to live? Then pay careful attention to

You know what I think was the one great thing I did? I went for it. I think that's the only thing I've done that was great.

Jon Stewart

We're all worms. But I do believe that I am a glowworm.

Winston Churchill

For me success has four parts: never stop learning, believe in yourself, even when no one else does, find a way to make a difference, and eat the heart of the watermelon.

Harvey B. Mackay

the following ten statements because they're not just words, they're secrets that many people have discovered and used to realize their dreams.

Top Ten Reasons You Can Get Your Dream Job

10. Ordinary people do extraordinary things.

9. People who achieve success rarely know how they'll accomplish it (they only believe it is possible).

8. You don't have to be twice as good as everyone else— just a little bit better.

7. "The secret of success is constancy of purpose." —*Benjamin Disraeli*

6. "The world stands aside to let anyone pass who knows where he or she is going." —*David Starr Jordan*

5. "Nothing will take you farther than persistence." —*Calvin Coolidge*

4. "Anything can be achieved by taking action, deciding what's working and what's not and changing the approach until you achieve what you want." —*Anthony Robbins*

3. "Luck favors the person who is going after their dreams." —*Richard Nelson Bolles*

2. "That the moment one definitely commits oneself then Providence moves too. All sorts of things occur to help one that would never otherwise have occurred." —*W. H. Murray*

1. If at first you don't succeed you're like everyone else who went on to greatness.

While I know many people who would testify to the truth of the ten reasons above, the best thing to do is confirm them for yourself. Try them out. Put them to work for you. Anything is possible if you just make a decision to take action and try your best.

CHAPTER 30

Choices That Pay Off

If only God would give me a sign . . .
like making a large deposit in my name
to a Swiss bank account.

Woody Allen

It has been three years since I wrote *Major in Success*, and this revised edition offers me an opportunity to share some more advice with you. The biggest thing I've learned in the last three years is that it's all about action. If you want extraordinary things to happen in your life, then put the suggested steps into action. Don't delay. Don't question whether they'll work for you. Just take action. Success isn't rocket science—it is a fantastic hike that you go on by moving your feet.

I feel enormously fortunate to have been able to become a professional speaker, and know that I got here primarily by taking the Action Steps and committing to the Six Habits suggested in this book. But there is another element that will play a part in your success: financial management. Take the story of art student Scott Leberecht, for example. Scott utilized smart financial management to enable him to meet the experts and geniuses who were responsible for the eye-popping scenes in such movies as *Star Wars* and *Jurassic Park*.

Scott walked the halls of the University of Cincinnati with a burning desire to work at the most prestigious special effects company in the world, Industrial Light and Magic. All of his heroes were moviemakers, and most of them worked at ILM; after all, it was founded and run by the creator of *Star Wars*, George Lucas. Scott held on to his dream throughout college, even after applying and being rejected for an ILM internship spring semester of his sophomore year.

I feel like I've had glimpses of how big life can be. I think trying to get a bigger perspective, trying to let go of things that limit your capacity is an ongoing effort. You can always be bigger.

Meg Ryan

153

One fateful day, Scott was walking down the hall on his way home from class, when he was stopped dead in his tracks by a poster that said, "The Making of Jurassic Park: Your opportunity to meet and learn from the pros who made the highest grossing movie ever." It was a four-day conference held during the summer in Hawaii.

"I couldn't believe my eyes. I desperately wanted to attend that conference," Scott recalls. "I knew I would meet people from ILM there. But it was 5,000 miles away and cost more than I had in the bank."

He dashed back to his residence-hall room and began figuring if he could somehow afford the trip. The first call he made was to a travel agent who informed him that he could get a low supersaver fare of $631, but only if he purchased his ticket by the next day. Scott was in a jam. He didn't have $631 to spare—and he wouldn't be able to earn that kind of money until midway through summer.

He figured and figured and figured, and it came down to this: The only way he'd be able to attend the conference was by charging it to his credit card and working a summer job to pay off the debt before the start of the next school year.

Scott remembers his decision well:

"I was Mr. Pay-It-Off-in-Full-at-the-End-of-the-Month because nobody was going to bail me out if I got in over my head. Charging this conference to my card not only meant I'd be going into debt, but also that I'd have to work a summer job and save my money—so I decided to think about my decision overnight. When I woke up the next morning, the first thought that raced through my mind was this statement that I'd read somewhere: 'It comes down to the question, What are you willing to sacrifice to get what you desire?' I was willing to sacrifice almost all my free time during the summer for a shot at ILM."

▶ **HOT TIP**

Stay away from 900 numbers that offer credit cards. They are usually scams.

Scott rolled out of bed and made two calls—one to his old boss lining up a summer job, and another to a travel agent to charge a ticket to Hawaii, on his credit card. Ninety-seven days later Scott was in Hawaii, mingling, shaking hands, and learning from the moviemaking superstars he'd read about since he was a kid.

"Being there made me realize that the people in Hollywood weren't as different as I thought. It gave me a sense that I could accomplish things similar to what they had accomplished," he recalls.

On top of the boost in confidence, Scott met many people who worked at ILM, and they gave him helpful hints for getting an internship at their company. Then, seven months after returning from the conference, Scott got the big payoff —an internship in the ILM art department. Even bigger than that, ten months after graduating from college, Scott was hired to be a full-time art director at ILM, and was soon working on Arnold Schwarzenegger's film *Eraser*.

Never keep up with the Joneses. Drag them down to your level. It's cheaper.

Quentin Crisp

To charge or not to charge?

While you are launching your career, it is also good to be establishing financial stability. Credit cards can be part of this process. While you are in college, you will be bombarded with credit card offers. People behind tables will offer you free gifts, if only you'll fill out a credit card application. Letters will pour into your mailbox that say "Because of your good credit history, you're preapproved with a $500 spending line." You may not have a "credit history," and you may not even have a job, but you will be able to get a credit card while you're in college. The point is, in college you'll probably have to decide if you want to apply for a credit card.

▶ **HOT TIP**

Always try to pay far more than the minimum payment due because most of the minimum goes toward interest charges only.

I remember getting my first credit card when I was in college. When I removed it from the envelope, I held it in my hand and looked at it with awe, realizing that, for the first time in my life, I could buy things now and pay for them later. But I opted to "freeload."

"Freeloading" is when you pay the entire amount due every month and, thus, avoid paying interest charges. In essence, this approach means you're using your card mostly for the convenience it gives you, for expenses you've got the cash to cover. That's a low-cost way to use a credit card. There is also another option. Nowadays you can get what is called a "debit card." Debit cards look like and can be used just like credit cards. Instead of loaning you money, however, they draw money directly out of your checking account. So if you've got enough money in your account, you can buy it with your debit card.

▶ **HOT TIP**

To ensure a good credit rating, pay your bills on time, never pay less than the required minimum, monitor your purchases, and budget to repay your debts.

There are three good reasons to use a debit card or a credit card while you're in college:

1. At times they are more convenient than a personal check, and they're often safer than cash.

2. Sometimes they are the only way to purchase an item (e.g., by the phone or through the Internet). For instance, try reserving a car without a credit card— sometimes possible, but extremely difficult.

3. Some cards offer you benefits on purchases made with your card, such as extended warranties, price protection guarantees, or airline travel miles.

Credit cards offer two benefits that debit cards do not:

1. They are an opportunity to establish a good credit rating that will benefit you after college (more on this later).

2. They can help you cover emergency expenses.

Use your credit card wisely and you'll have a very beneficial financial tool. Use your card unwisely and you'll end up in a financial nightmare. Some college students make the mistake of running up a credit card debt they can't afford. Nothing is easier than charging small things here and there, only to wake up some day and find yourself staring at a credit card bill, in your name, that says "Balance Due: $2,000." I chose the amount of $2,000 because that's the amount a freshman student in Texas named Michelle Raimey ran up in one semester. It took Michelle seven years to pay off the balance—and her parents weren't about to help, even though they had the money. It was a hard lesson for Michelle to learn, but one that she says "taught me the lesson that credit cards are in no way easy money."

Credit cards can be easy if, and only if, you follow these Twelve Brilliant Ways to Avoid a Credit Card Migraine:

1. No matter what, PAY YOUR MONTHLY CREDIT CARD BILL ON TIME. Come hell or high water, pay it on time, even if all you can pay is the minimum amount due, because you'll protect your credit rating, and you'll avoid late fees that are often as much as $20.

2. Keep a written record of every charge you make with your card, as if you were Scrooge himself. Use the record to stay within your budget.

▶ **HOT TIP**

If you find a mistake on your credit card bill, immediately write a letter to your card issuer and clearly describe the problem. Keep a record of your communication to your issuer. You have rights.

▶ **HOT TIP**

There is a free list on the Web that names some of the lowest rate and lowest fee cards: cardweb.com/cardtrack/main.html

Perhaps there is only one cardinal sin: impatience. Because of impatience we are driven out of Paradise; because of impatience we cannot return.
Franz Kafka

3. Limit yourself to one credit card. Two simply increase the odds of screwing up.

4. Avoid impulse purchases. Spontaneity and credit cards are a bad mix. Consider the purchase for a couple of days and do the right (fiscally smart) thing. Remember to calculate the REAL cost of your desired purchase: A $100 jacket doesn't cost $100 if you charge it to your card and take six months to pay it off. It costs $100 + six months of interest.

5. Reward yourself in no-cost ways. Just because you aced all your finals doesn't mean you deserve something you can't afford. Instead of spending money you don't have, blast a stereo and stay up all night with a friend.

6. Avoid shopping as entertainment.

7. Don't charge beyond your budget for holidays, which is when most people blow it.

8. Pay your credit card bill first, before you spend your money on everything else. Having a perfect payment history with your credit card is important.

9. Pay close attention to notices from your credit card company. Sometimes they are announcing a higher interest rate or new fees. If you don't like the new terms, get a new card and transfer your balance.

10. Don't use your credit card for cash advances. Cash advances are far more expensive than normal charges. They have higher interest rates, additional fees, and typically no grace period.

11. Treat your credit card like a $1,000 bill. Protect it from theft.

12. Refuse to load up on debt. Because of the way interest charges are calculated, if you're not careful, you may find yourself in a snowball situation.

Danger! Danger! Danger!

If you don't use your credit cards wisely, you'll find yourself in financial ruin. Nothing is easier, or happens faster, than running up a credit card to an astronomical sum and then not being able to make your minimum monthly payment (when you run up $5,000 of debt, your monthly minimums can be

▶ **HOT TIP**

You can get a copy of your credit rating upon request. The cost is at most $8, varying from state to state.
- Experian! 1-800-392-1122
- Equifax Information Service Center: 1.800.685.1111
- TransUnion Corporation: 1.800.916.8800

▶ **HOT TIP**

Notify your credit card companies when you move so that your bills will still arrive on time and you can pay them on time.

▶ **HOT TIP**

Landlords often look at your credit report to choose among rental applicants—so always pay your bills on time.

right around \$200). If you can't make the monthly minimum, then the ceiling comes crashing down on you. Suddenly, you'll be overwhelmed with debt, you won't be able to take vacations because you'll have to work just to pay your debt, you'll have a bad credit rating, and no one will rent you an apartment, loan you money, or sell you a car. Suddenly, you'll have no CreditAbility.

CreditAbility

You have a credit rating and people (including yourself) can access it through several sources. Before you own a credit card, your credit rating is based on how responsibly you manage your checking account, monthly bills in your name, and any retail credit accounts you may have, including gasoline cards. Student loans and car loans also affect your credit rating. But, once you own a credit card, your credit rating becomes based largely on how responsibly you manage your credit card.

Building a great credit rating shows you are financially responsible. After you graduate, it should be easier for you to buy big-ticket items that often require a loan, such as a house, a car, or a boat. Some day, you may even want to use your good credit to borrow seed money to start your own business. Remember, while building a good credit rating is important, at the same time, you want to avoid anything that negatively affects that rating (such as missing or late payments). Good credit takes toooo long to establish not to use it wisely.

There are additional consequences for having a sloppy payment history. Gone are the credit line increases when you

As Miss America, my goal is to bring peace to the entire world and then to get my own apartment.

Jay Leno

▶ **HOT TIP**

Employers often look at your credit report as a way to help them decide whether to hire you—so always pay your bills on time.

▶ **HOT TIP**

Never write your credit card number on your check. You are not obligated to give the merchant this information.

need them, "No Annual Fee!" offers, and the low-interest rate offers. Mess up, and you will be saddled with the worst credit card terms known to man.

Signs that you are getting into credit card trouble:

- You don't know how much you owe until your bills arrive.
- You're using credit card cash advances to pay bills.
- You're getting calls or letters from your creditors about overdue bills.
- You're often paying your bills late.
- Your credit cards are being revoked.
- You're only paying the minimum payment required.
- Your pulse quickens when you total up your debt.

More words of advice: Each month, pay more than the minimum payment to avoid paying more in the end. Robert McKinley, president of RAM Research, offers this cautionary example: Let's say you owe $2,000 on a credit card that charges 18% interest, and you make the minimum 2% payment every month. It would take more than 30 years to pay off the debt, and you'd be paying about three to four times the original balance. Yowza!

If you find yourself in credit card trouble, the best solution is to immediately pick up the phone and get help. Call your credit card company and tell them the truth about your situation because they will often help you with a payment plan. Or call Consumer Credit Counseling Services (CCCS) at 1-800-388-2227. CCCS is a national nonprofit organization that can help you maintain a good credit standing with your creditors. They can work with creditors to restructure a payment plan. Best of all, CCCS's services are usually FREE!

Having said all that, you know how to stay out of credit card trouble. Next, you're about to discover how to choose the best credit card. All credit cards are not created equal. Some super, super expensive cards may appear to be cheap ones.

▶ **HOT TIP**

There is no reason for a merchant to require you to provide your phone number and address as a condition of making a purchase with your credit card.

Put all your eggs in one basket and WATCH THAT BASKET!

Mark Twain

▶ **HOT TIP**

Don't use your credit card to pay for 900 numbers unless you're filthy rich—no matter how low the "advertised rate" is, 900 calls are always super expensive.

A Gallup survey shows that handling an emergency situation is the #1 reason Americans carry credit cards.

The price of not following your dream is the same as paying for it.

Paulo Coelho

The super-smart way to choose your credit card

First, you want to choose your credit card instead of letting a card choose you. Decide the terms you want and shop for those terms. This is generally what you're looking for in a credit card:

1. If you're certain that you'll pay off your balance every month, and I mean CERTAIN, then get a card with no annual fee, and a 25- to 30-day grace period on purchases.

2. If you might carry a balance owed from month to month, then go for a card with a low interest rate and low or no annual fee. Interest rate offers range between 9% and 19%.

3. The final consideration can be the special benefits and rewards a card offers. But watch out, because the best reward programs may come with the cards that have the higher fees and interest rates. Those special "extras" ain't free.

CAUTION!

You'll receive a lot of offers that say, "Low Introductory Interest Rate!" These offers mean your interest rate will be really low at first, but after a while it will go up A LOT. Your job is to find out: (1) When the interest rate will go up and (2) what the interest rate will go up to. To answer these questions, call the credit card company extending the offer and ask. An introductory period that lasts nine months to a year is good, and so is an interest rate that won't exceed about 14%. *Remember, choose the credit card terms you want, don't let them choose you.*

"Payback Potential"

Most items that students charge to their credit cards are often items they *want* such as a stereo or TV, clothes, jewelry, $100 tennis shoes, food and drink, CDs, home furnishings, or 900 numbers. You can keep your debt down by only charging things you actually *need* to your card. To the degree that you can want less material items, to that degree you are wealthy. It can be hard not to buy many things you want, but in the words of Bernard Baruch, "In the last analysis, our only freedom is the freedom to discipline ourselves." If you come to a point where you are going to acquire debt on your credit card and spend beyond your current means, think about only charging items that you *need*, or that have payback potential.

What are expenses with "payback potential"? They are expenses you incur now that will help you make money in the near future, such as:

- Quality portfolio materials
- Tools for your trade
- Career books
- Workshops, trade shows, and conferences
- Computer hardware and software
- Office supplies
- A nice business suit
- Business cards
- Subscriptions to trade journals and newsletters

▶ **HOT TIP**

Lost or stolen card? Call your card issuer. If you don't know the phone number, call directory assistance at 800-555-1212 and ask for your card issuer's 800 number.

▶ **HOT TIP**

Free online credit seminar at creditinfocenter.com

▶ **HOT TIP**

Never write your PIN down and keep it in your wallet.

▶ **HOT TIP**

Don't pay one credit card bill with a cash advance from another. If you're at this point, call your credit card issuer for help.

When you've dug yourself into a hole, stop digging.
Old Texas Saying

Takes money to make money

Most of the time it does take money to make money. So if you find yourself in a place where money is truly a necessary tool for carving out your career, and you don't have a friend, relative, or a financial institution that will loan you money, a credit card will do the trick. But you must follow these Three Rules for Powerful Plastic Use:

1. Only charge things that have "payback potential." Rather than spending on items you want, shift to only spending on items you need—items that have a direct correlation to furthering your career. Use your card to empower yourself to be a success. Then, later you'll have the income to afford the things you want.

2. Keep your interest rate as low as possible. Call your credit card company and ask them to lower your interest rate. If you have a good credit rating, and mention a competing offer, they often will lower your interest rate—just because you asked.

3. Sacrifice, work, and discipline yourself until your dreams come true and your debt is paid off. Don't ever assume that paying off your debt will be easy—assume you will be able to do it with a focused and committed effort.

True power and extraordinary results

Three years ago I knew the steps I was suggesting in this book worked, but now I understand that their power to create extraordinary results cannot be underestimated. Because I took the Action Steps and committed to the Six Habits, my career has taken off and I constantly feel like shouting, "I did it! I did it! I did it!" I actually carved out a career for myself doing something I truly enjoy, truly am grateful to do, and wouldn't trade for the world. And, the rewards keep getting bigger and bigger.

In one of my all-time favorite books, *The Alchemist*, author Paulo Coelho teaches that everyone on Earth has a treasure that awaits them, and that, "When you're searching for your treasure, you'll discover things along the way you'd never have discovered had you not had the courage to try for things that seemed impossible for you." Begin searching for your treasure now. Dream big. Take action. Develop successful habits, and be great. Becoming successful is easier than

> **▶ HOT TIP**
> Never give your credit card number to a caller who says he needs it to award you a free trip or prize. Figure it's probably a scam.

> **▶ HOT TIP**
> The book *Get a Financial Life*, by Beth Kobliner

> **▶ HOT TIP**
> *Personal Finance for Dummies* by Eric Tyson

> I will never give in until the day that I die. I'll get myself some independence, carve out a future with my two bare hands.
> *Lyrics from the song "Spirit of '76" by The Alarm*

> And will you succeed? Yes! You will indeed! (98 and ¾ percent guaranteed.)
> *Dr. Seuss, from Oh, the Places You'll Go!*

most people make it out to be, and dreams really do come true.

Never underestimate what you can do during college. College students have launched almost every kind of business under the sun, from health food stores to clothing companies. College students have starred in movies and commercials, written best-selling books, published ground-breaking research, shot photos for national publications, launched successful record labels, and on and on. The majority of students will just study, test, study, and test. But, some people, possibly yourself included, will add to the list of incredible things college students have done—and it won't be a miracle, or luck, or good fortune. It will happen because a student went for it.

- College students launched Microsoft.

- College students made the smash-hit film *The Blair Witch Project.*

- College students revolutionized the world by programming the first web browser, Mosaic (which was the precursor to Netscape Navigator).

- College students have written hit movies such as *Goodwill Hunting* and *Boyz N the Hood.*

- A college student started FedEx.

- A college student wrote a report that landed her on *Larry King Live,* earned her a six-figure publishing deal, and impacted the U.S. Senate.

- A college student launched Dell Computers.

- A college student booked Bill Cosby to speak at an event for thousands.

- A college student discovered the band *Live* and managed them to many #1 hits.

- A college student launched the nationwide nonprofit organization Teach for America.

- College students have created some of the most popular Internet sites in the world including Yahoo, theGlobe.com, and Collegeclub.com.

- A college student launched the city newspaper in Madison, Connecticut.

- A college student launched Aardvark Studios, which shoots photos of millions of graduating high school seniors.

Go for it—you've got what it takes.

Beat the System's Imperfections

- The system said Elvis was an F student in music. Beat the system by believing in yourself more than you believe in the grades your professors give you.

- The system says G.P.A. is an important indicator of your future success. Know that G.P.A. rarely affects a student's life outside of academia.

- The system says you'll get kicked out if you don't pass. Comply with the system by at least passing your classes because, like it or not, a college degree *does* make a difference.

- The system says you are in school for pure academics. Remember to get some real-life work experience along with your schooling.

- The system says your selection of a major is all-important. Select the major that you're passionate about and pursue whatever career sounds most enjoyable.

- The system says go to class and learn. Learn from everywhere—classes, clubs, leadership programs, internships, mentors, friends, books, TV, and overseas programs.

- The system says professors can teach you best. Remember that no one can teach you better than yourself or another successful person. Learn from the best, someone who's already achieved things you want to achieve.

- The system says that only some people are creative. Be creative in everything you do.

- The system says your credentials determine what you can be. Do anything you want to do and don't let "credentials" stand in your way.

- The system says there are no shortcuts. Meet successful people, read success books, and find your own kind of shortcuts.

- The system says getting somewhere is important. Aim for somewhere, but remember to enjoy every step of the way.

- The system says you're here to prepare for the next test. Prepare for a successful and satisfying life. Make your *own* agenda.

Bonus Appendix

Bonus Tips for Teachers, Artists, Exchange Students, and Athletes

Teachers

Everything in *Major in Success* applies to teachers, and in particular, you'll benefit from knowing these five things: First, two teaching credentials make you twice as valuable. Second, if you've been involved in a campus club, or in a sport, you will be much more likely to be hired because you're more valuable if you can help run student activities or coach a sport. Third, computers are everywhere in schools so being good with computers is essential. Fourth, being bilingual is so helpful to teachers. And finally, do a lot of extracurriculars that will demonstrate to a school administrator that you truly enjoy working with kids, i.e., working in a day-care center, being involved with kids through your church, running a Girl Scouts' club.

Hot tip for teachers: Call (847) 864-1999 and get a copy of *The Job Search Handbook for Educators* if you're going into the K–12 environment. If you're going to teach in higher education, you want *The Higher Education Job Search* (aaee.org).

Artists

This book was written with you very much in mind, especially since artists are aiming for very cool jobs. Add these five philosophies to your approach to success: First, the biggest mistake most art students make after graduating is they come up with noncreative solutions to the pragmatic problem of survival, like waiting tables 50 hours a week so they can afford to live in New York City. Noncreative solutions like this will drain your creative spirit. You will have a much better and more rewarding life if you solve your challenges of survival creatively, like living in New Jersey where the rent is much less and commuting into New York City. Teaching kids to finger paint for part-time work is more creative than waiting tables. Second, don't stay on the fence trying to decide whether you'll stick with the arts or not. The indecision is a big waste of energy. Simply decide to commit to it for five years. You'll be amazed at how this frees up your mind to think creatively. Third, stay in touch with friends in the arts. You'll meet other artists in school and after school. Cultivate these relationships. Be a great networker. Artists often rise together. Artists you know will succeed and need a director for their play, need to fill a gallery space, need to recommend another actor. If you've cultivated these relationships your lucky breaks will come much more often. Fourth, create a lifestyle with the lowest money needs possible. This will take a lot of pressure off. And finally, the arts, although often restrictive in money and security, have so much to offer for people who truly value creativity and individuality. So, in the words of Jim Petosa, artistic director of the Olney Theatre in Washington D.C., "If you're not going to enjoy the tremendous liberated feeling afforded by being in the arts, then don't do it."

Hot Tips for Artists

Check out these books:

Careers for Music Lovers & Other Tuneful Types (VGM Publishing)

Opportunities in Performing Arts Careers (VGM Publishing)

Opportunities in Visual Arts Careers (VGM Publishing)

The Working Actors Guide to Los Angeles (Aaron Blake Publishing) 800-729-6423

These Web sites:

- franklinquest.com/priorities/vol2issu3_career.html (A great on-line article about networking.)

- http://ca.yahoo.com/Arts/Performing_Arts/Theater/Magazines (Especially good are BackStage.com, an awesome site about NYC theater, and the sites about regional community theater.)

- artjob.org (A great source for jobs in the visual arts.)

- westaf.org (An awesome source of links for visual artists and independent film makers.)

- artswire.org (An online community for the arts. Great for links and connections in the art world.)

- concertartists.org (The Concert Artists Guild site for musicians. They publish a great book about music competitions.)

- dramaguild.com (The Dramatists Guild Web site.)

- theatredirectories.com

Exchange Students

Check out these sites. ciee.org has an awesome database that lists internships and seasonal jobs in the U.S. for exchange students. worldclub.org is a site for exchange students and has many resources and links.

Athletes

The question I get most often from athletes is, "How can I fit in things like a semester overseas, campus clubs, and internships? Sports take up all my free time." I answer with a story. An exceptional college athlete I met, Ben Wittowski, ran track year-round, devoting at least twenty hours to sports every week. He also fit in a twenty-hour-a-week internship, during three different semesters—one with a sports agent, one promoting his school's Midnight Madness event, and another for a professor, helping to promote the university's baseball games. His grades were excellent during these busy times. However, interestingly, the semester that he only did school and track, his grades went down. He told me it left him with too much time on his hands and his time management suffered all around. There is research to back up what Ben discovered on his own. Studies have confirmed that with a lot to do, people really use their time well and do better in all their activities. People with extra time, on the other hand, feel less urgency and end up squandering valuable time away. Their performance suffers as a result. The second question I get from athletes is, "If I don't make it as a professional athlete, what should I do?" I stick with the philosophy of "follow your bliss." Consider following your passion for sports into a sports industry job. The books below will turn you on to the many job options for people with a passion for sports:

Careers for Sports Nuts & Other Athletic Types by William Ray Heitzmann

The 50 Coolest Jobs in Sports: Who's Got Them, What They Do, and How You Can Get One! by David Fischer

The Guide to Careers in Sports by Leonard Karlin

You Can't Play the Game If You Don't Know the Rules: Career Opportunities in Sports Management by David M. Carter

Career Opportunities in the Sports Industry by Shelly Field

Sports Market Place: Guide to over 10,000 Sports Organizations, Teams, Corporate Sponsors, Sports Agents, Marketing and Event Management Agencies, Media, Manufacturers and Retailers, edited by Richard Lipsey, ISBN 0-935644-02-4 (Look for this one in your library because it sells for $199.)

jobsinsports.com has job listings, but has a monthly subscription fee.

Web Sites for Success

JOB AND CAREER SITES

backdoorjobs.com

careerbuilder.com

careermag.com

careerplanit.com

collegegrad.com

fastcompany.com/career/find.html

hiredmag.com

internjobs.com

jobdirect.com

jobhuntersbible.com

jobsourcenetwork.com

jobweb.com

powerstudents.com

resortjobs.com/

review.com/career/topten.cfm

summerjobs.com

PROFESSIONAL ASSOCIATIONS AND SOCIETIES

asae.com

www.lib.uwaterloo.ca/society/
overview.html

ON-LINE PERSONAL CAREER COACHES

careerdiscovery.com

PATRICK COMBS SITES (FREE NEWSLETTER SIGN-UP)

goodthink.com

patrickcombs.com

ON-LINE NETWORKING

planetall.com

sixdegrees.com

VOLUNTEERING

americaspromise.org

americorps.org

city-year.org

impactonline.org,

servenet.org,

strength.org

ARTICLES FOR MORE INFORMATION

- Networking:
  franklinquest.com/priorities/
  vol2issu3_career.html
- Internet job hunting:
  franklinquest.com/priorities/
  vol2issu2_internet.html
- Entreprenuering:
  franklinquest.com/priorities/
  vol2issu1_career.html
- Time management:
  franklinqust.com/organizational/
  knowledge/lib/first.html

FRIENDS OF PATRICK COMBS

deannalatson.com

onlineconsulting.com

rawfood.com

totalsuccess.com

About the Author

College Attended

Lewis & Clark College for a year and a half, then went on to graduate from San Francisco State University with a B.A. in speech and communications.

Job Title

Ambitious talker and beginning writer.

What I Really Do

All I seem to do is redo: redo my speech; rewrite a chapter; redo a brochure; rethink my business. Computers make redoing much easier so most of the time my hands are on a keyboard. On my "days out" I get to go to colleges to speak.

Why I Do It

Have always wanted to have an unusual job. Always admired public speakers. Like to be able to play guitar while I'm at work. Love to read about success traits. Don't want a boss. Figured I could make a great salary. As for why I write—at first because I figured it would help my speaking. I was surprised to find that I enjoy it.

What I Did Before

Couple of summers ago I was video game tester.

Before that for two years I was producer of a highly acclaimed multimedia event about leadership called *A Day in the Future.*

My first job out of college was at Levi Strauss & Co., first as an intern and then later as videoconferencing manager.

During college I managed a great rock band called the Square Roots. (They broke up, though.)

Most Loved Movie Experience

Defending Your Life by Albert Brooks (No Fear!) and *The Matrix.*

Best Fast Food

Fruit.

Dreams and Ambitions

Being the best public speaker I know of; making funny and informative films for television; taking songwriting lessons from Ray Davies; writing a book as good as *How to Win Friends and Influence People;* getting to go to one of the other planets.

My Heroes

Ray Davies of the Kinks, Will Rogers, Muhammad Ali, and Ferris Bueller (to name a few).

Blast from the Past

Outward Bound for 21 days in the Desert. Check it out: www.goodthink.com/out-wardbound.html

What I Think Life Is All About

Trying to figure out what life is all about.

Favorite Quote

"I used to work at the International House of Pancakes. It was a dream, and I made it happen."—Paula Poundstone, comedian

More ways to major in success

Speeches

Patrick Combs is one of the college cir-
cuit's most popular speakers. You, as a student, have the power to help bring him to
your school—more power and influence
than you probably are aware of. To learn
more about how you can influence what
speakers your school invites, and earn a
$100 reward, contact the Good Thinking
Co., 3707 Fifth Avenue PMB 140, San
Diego, CA 92103-4221. (619) 291-4743.
Info@goodthink.com
(www.goodthink.com).

Video

Patrick Combs's motivational speech is
available on video. It's a 60-minute speech
recorded live. The cost is $49.00. To order,
contact: Good Thinking Co. (619) 291-
4743. Info@goodthink.com.

Patrick Combs's Web Site

Visit Patrick's Web sites. You'll find weekly
columns by Patrick, stories about Patrick's
career, and free articles on success, inspirational quotes, and success stories. Sign up
to receive Patrick's free newsletter.

- www.goodthink.com & patrick-
  combs.com
- E-mail Patrick Combs your com-
  ments, suggestions, success stories,
  and questions: pcombs@good-
  think.com

Do Other Students a Favor

If you have some good words to say about
Major in Success, please post your review of
the book at Amazon.com and bn.com.
You'll be helping more students turn on to
this book.

Want to be super-successful on your first job?

Provide Patrick with answers to the following five questions and he will send you a FREE special report normally sold for $10.00 called HOW TO BE TWICE AS SUCCESSFUL ON YOUR FIRST JOB OR INTERNSHIP.

1. Who are you?

Name:
Address:
Phone:
E-mail:
Age:
Year in school:
Major:

2. How did you become aware that this book even existed?

☐ saw it in a bookstore
☐ someone recommended it to me
☐ saw an advertisement for it
☐ attended Patrick's lecture
☐ heard about it on the radio
☐ heard about it on TV
☐ received it as a gift from my parents
☐ learned about it at Patrick's Web site (www.goodthink.com)
☐ none of the above. I heard about it by_____

3. What is your opinion of this book?

4. Does Patrick have permission to quote you?

☐ yes
☐ no

5. What changes would you suggest for future editions?

Thanks for your truthful answers. Honest and sincere feedback allows Patrick to improve his work. For your FREE special report, e-mail the above information to pcombs@goodthink.com, or mail this form and a SELF-ADDRESSED, STAMPED ENVELOPE to:

Patrick Combs
Good Thinking Co.
3707 Fifth Avenue PMB 140
San Diego, CA 92103-4221

Order Form

- Fax orders: (619) 295-2779
- Telephone orders: Call toll free: (888) 429-5290. Have your AMEX, Discover, VISA, or Mastercard ready.
- On-line orders: www.goodthink.com/bookback.html

Please send _____ **copies of** *Major in Success:*

I understand that I may return any book for a full refund—for any reason, no questions asked.

Company name: _____

Name: _____

Address: _____

City: _____ State: _____ Zip: _____ – _____

Telephone: (_____) _____

Sales tax:
Please add 7.75% for books shipped to California addresses.

Shipping:
$3.00 for the first book and $2.00 for each additional book.

Payment:

___ Check

___ Credit card: ___ VISA ___ Mastercard ___ AMEX ___ Discover

Card number: _____

Name on card: _____ Exp. Date: _____ / _____

Call *toll free* and order now